GROWING UP INTO CHRIST

By

Rev. Larry L. Eddings
Copyright, 2012, Revised 2018
All Rights Reserved

ACKNOWLEDGMENTS

The preparation and publication of a book requires the research, counsel and wisdom of individuals who have expertise in that field of study. It also requires evidence in lives that validate the truth of that which is contained in the book.

The Word of God, as contained in Holy Scripture, is foundational to Truth. Jesus prayed, *"Sanctify them by the truth. Thy Word is Truth."* John 17:17. I wish to acknowledge the absolute Truth of God's Word upon which this book is based. The New Revised Standard Version of the Holy Bible is the primary Scripture that is used, unless otherwise noted.

I acknowledge the wise counsel and examples of certain lay persons and colleagues in ministry who have been living examples of how the Holy Spirit works in the lives of individuals who desire to become mature disciples of Jesus Christ:

Special acknowledgment must be made to The Rev. Dr. Tom Albin, Dean of The Upper Room of the General Board of Discipleship of The United Methodist Church, at the time of this writing, who took the time to read the manuscript and make valuable notations that greatly improve the accuracy, clarity and message contained therein.

Jack and Ruby Langill, lay persons, and other saints in the United Methodist Church in Silverdale, WA, who were used by God to help me learn to live, grow and walk in the Spirit;

Dr. Ross Whetstone, first Executive Director of Aldersgate Renewal Ministries, formerly United Methodist Renewal Fellowship Services, who encouraged my extended participation in the greater move of the Holy Spirit through the Renewal Ministries of the larger Church.

Dr. Joe Harding, a beloved colleague in ministry, now with the Lord in heaven, with whom I served in local conferences and whose life and ministry challenged me to reach beyond my natural skills and call on the power of the Holy Spirit, boldly proclaiming the Gospel of our Lord, Jesus Christ.

Students, and others, in the various classes where the material was taught and who made valuable contributions in discussions and suggestions for practical refinement and application in a Believer's daily life;

To you, the readers of this book, who have a continuing desire to Grow Up in Christ and become mature in your discipleship. May you and I always have the passion and burning desire to "Walk in the dust of our Rabbi, Jesus"

TABLE OF CONTENTS

Acknowledgments

Introduction   5

Chapter 1 – Born of the Spirit   8

Chapter 2 – Growing in the Spirit   18

Chapter 3 – Baptized with the Spirit   27

Chapter 4 – Led by the Spirit   39

Chapter 5 – Empowered by the Spirit   53

Chapter 6 – Anointed by the Spirit   69

Chapter 7 – Resurrected by the Spirit   77

Chapter 8 – Mature in the Spirit   88

Bibliography

SCRIPTURE

"The gifts he [Jesus] gave were that some would be apostles, some prophets, some evangelists, some pastors and teachers, to equip the saints for the work of ministry, for building up the body of Christ, until all of us come to the unity of the faith and of the knowledge of the Son of God, to maturity, to the measure of the full stature of Christ.

"We must no longer be children, tossed to and fro and blown about by every wind of doctrine, by people's trickery, by their craftiness in deceitful scheming. But speaking the truth in love, we must grow up in every way into him who is the head, into Christ, from whom the whole body, joined and knit together by every ligament with which it is equipped, as each part is working properly promotes the body's growth in building itself up in love."

Ephesians 4:11-16
New Revised Standard Version of the Bible

INTRODUCTION

"Aw, grow up and act you age," the older sister yelled out at her brother. This appears to be a favorite give and take among siblings who are in the growing up process, especially when a younger one is pestering or teasing an older one. Even though usually spoken as a verbal, sarcastic attack – or counterattack, there is truth embedded in the statements. It is indeed desirable that a person "grow up" and "act their age" when it comes to personal behavior, though perhaps it would be more productive if the words were spoken as an encouragement rather than a "put down."

Christians in the early Church were encouraged to "grow up," "act their age" and become mature in their beliefs, in their behavior and in their commitments. The truth is, newly born Christians cannot remain spiritual infants. When the apostle Paul wrote to the church in Ephesus, he included in that letter instructions for them, regarding how they were to grow up and mature in their faith. He wrote,

*"It is he [Christ] who gave some to be apostles, some to be prophets, some to be evangelists, and some to be pastors and teachers, to prepare God's people for works of service, so that the body of Christ may be built up until we all reach unity in the faith and in the knowledge of the Son of God and **become mature, attaining to the whole measure of the fullness of Christ**. Then we will no longer be infants, tossed back and forth by the waves, and blown here and there by every wind of teaching and by the cunning and craftiness of men in their deceitful scheming. Instead, we will in all things grow up into him who is the head, that is, Christ. From him the whole body, joined and held together by every supporting ligament, grows and builds itself up in love, as each part does its work."* [Ephesians 4:11-16, NIV, with author's **emphasis** added]

A car, traveling on a modern highway, displayed the personalized license plate which read, YGROWUP. The answer to that question for the Christian is clear: our goal as the Church, individually and collectively, according to Paul, is to become mature, *"to the measure of the full stature of Christ."* We are to *"grow up in every way into Him who is the Head, into Christ."*

As Christians, we are to be like Jesus Christ. If we are to experience the whole measure of the fullness of Christ, what happened in the life of Jesus can and must also happen in our lives.

Scripture reminds us that *"Jesus is the reflection of God's glory and the exact imprint of God's very being."* [Hebrews 1:3] The greatest revelation of God's plan for humanity is seen in the life of Jesus.

God was pleased to have all his fullness dwell in Jesus and through Jesus, God has moved to bring reconciliation between creation and God's own self. [Colossians 1:19, 20]

From Jesus we learn the way in which God's Spirit works to restore a fallen humanity to the original vision that God had for it before the foundation of the world. Jesus is the 'role model' who enables us to see what God has in mind for us.

Jesus told his disciples, *"A disciple is not above the teacher, nor a slave above the master; it is enough for the disciple to be like the teacher, and the slave like the master."* [Matthew 10:24, 25] Jesus intended for his followers to be like him.

In Orthodox Judaism of Jesus' day, students were told, "May you be covered in the dust of your Rabbi." The thought behind this was that as a rabbi walked the dusty roads of Israel, his chosen disciples would follow close behind him, so closely that they would get covered with the dust of their Rabbi.

The disciple [*talmid*] wanted to be so much like his Rabbi that when the Rabbi did anything the disciple would imitate it. When he sat, the disciple sat. When the Rabbi ate, the disciple ate. When the Rabbi taught, the disciple listened. What the Rabbi taught, the disciple taught. The *talmid* desired more than anything to be like his Rabbi.

A Rabbis' disciples were identified by the actions and teachings that reflected those of their Rabbi. Jesus told his disciples, *"By this all men will know that you are my disciples, if you love one another."* John 13:35

The disciple of Jesus desires to "walk in the dust" of his or her Rabbi, Jesus. They desire more than anything to be like him.; to manifest his love.

This image is reflected in the relationship between Jesus and his Father, God. At one point in his ministry he said, *"I tell you the truth, the Son can do nothing by himself; he can do only what he sees his Father doing, because whatever the Father does, the Son also does,"* and *"Whatever I say is just what the Father has told me to say."* [John 12:49, 50] Jesus stayed close to the Father and whatever his disciples saw him do and say, was exactly what the Father told him to do and say.

Just as Jesus is the *"reflection of God's glory and the exact imprint of God's very being,"* [Hebrews 1:3], the Holy Spirit enables us to be "the reflection of Jesus' glory and the exact imprint of Jesus' very being." It is the Holy Spirit who helps us stay close enough to Jesus to be like Jesus and "be covered with his dust."

The Holy Spirit of God is the Person of the Triune Godhead who enables us, as individual disciples of Jesus as well as the corporate Church, to grow up in our faith and become mature, *"attaining to the full measure of the stature of Christ."*

God's Holy Spirit in the life of Jesus, the man, reveals the mystery of God's plan regarding the restoration of humanity to a right, good and perfect relationship with its Creator.

According to Scripture, the Holy Spirit has a seven-fold nature.

> *"Grace and peace to you from Him who is and who was, and who is to come and from the sevenfold Spirit before His throne, and from Jesus Christ, who is the faithful witness, the firstborn from the dead, and the ruler of the kings of the earth."* [Revelation 1:4, 5, NIV]

In speaking of the Holy Spirit, "sevenfold" may mean complete and whole. It may also mean the many functions or works of the Spirit of God. Both meanings may be seen in the life of Jesus. Both may be seen in the way that the Spirit works in the life of a person to bring them into wholeness in their relationship with God.

Both may be seen in the way the Spirit works to grow us up in our faith and bring us to maturity in Jesus Christ. Both may be seen in how the Spirit brings us to *"attain to the full measure of the stature of Christ."*

It is important, then, that we understand how the Holy Spirit worked in the life of Jesus as he walked here on earth, so that we can be open to allowing the Spirit to work in the same, or very similar ways in our lives.

The following pages are designed to help us understand how the Holy Spirit worked in Jesus' life from conception to resurrection; and how we can allow the Holy Spirit to accomplish the same work in our lives, thereby enabling us to become mature in our faith, attaining to the whole measure of the fullness of Christ, and grow up into Him who is our Head.

CHAPTER 1

BORN OF THE SPIRIT

"In the sixth month [Elul], the angel Gabriel was sent by God to a town in Galilee called Nazareth, to a virgin engaged to a man whose name was Joseph, of the house of David. The virgin's name was Mary. And he came to her and said, "Greetings, favored one! The Lord is with you."

But she was much perplexed by his words and pondered what sort of greeting this might be. The angel said to her, "Do not be afraid, Mary, for you have found favor with God. And now, you will conceive in your womb and bear a son, and you will name him Jesus. He will be great and will be called the Son of the Most High, and the Lord God will give to him the throne of his ancestor David. He will reign over the house of Jacob forever and of his kingdom there will be no end."

Mary said to the angel, "How can this be, since I am a virgin?"

The angel said to her, "The Holy Spirit will come upon you, and the power of the Most High will overshadow you; therefore, the child to be born will be holy; he will be called Son of God." Luke 1:26-35

The angel Gabriel was sent by God to Nazareth to a young woman named Mary [Miriam] to tell her,

"The Holy Spirit will come upon you, and the power of the Most High will overshadow you. Therefore, the child to be born will be holy; he will be called Son of God." Luke 1:35

Jesus' Physical and Spiritual Birth

Jesus was **conceived** by the Holy Spirit. One of the most beautiful and dramatic stories in Scripture is that of the conception and birth of Jesus. The Birth story is found in the Gospels of Matthew, chapter 1 and Luke, chapters 1 and 2.

Joseph and Mary, a Jewish man and woman, were betrothed to be married. The engagement began with the payment of fifty shekels [about $40.00 U.S. currency] to Mary's father as compensation for the loss of his daughter.

Friends of Mary had given her engagement parties where gifts were presented to her and she began collecting her trousseau.

Joseph was exempted from military service during that first year, according to the Jewish Law, so that he could prepare a home for his prospective bride and himself. [Deuteronomy 20:7, 24:5]

The wedding could happen only after the home had been prepared and Joseph's father, Jacob, Jesus' grandfather, said that it was adequate for him and his new bride. Only the groom's father could declare when the home was ready. When Joseph had the place ready and it passed his father's inspection, then his marriage to Mary could be consummated.

After a feast of joyous celebration, Mary and Joseph could live together as husband and wife, even though the community considered them 'married' during the engagement. If Joseph had died during the engagement, Mary would have been considered a widow.

It was during this time of betrothal that the angel of the Lord came to Mary and said, "Mary, you are going to have a baby." Under normal circumstances this would be the greatest of news for a Hebrew woman, for to give birth to a child is looked upon as a supreme blessing from God. To be barren is considered a judgment from God and a source of great shame.

Since Joseph and Mary's marriage had not yet been consummated, her response to the announcement of the angel is quite normal, "How can this be? I do not have a husband."

Mary was troubled, and so was Joseph when she told him. Joseph knew he was not the child's father. He knew also that under Jewish Law both he and Mary could be put to death. In cases of seduction, both the man and woman were put to death. [Deuteronomy 22:23, 24] In cases of forced relations, the man would be put to death. [Deuteronomy 22:25, 27]

Here is a young man and woman making normal plans for their future when suddenly confronted by the fact that she is expecting a child and they could both lose their lives because Sacred Law forbids it. Joseph determined quietly to break off the relationship with Mary.

However, amid his anxiety, the angel of the Lord spoke to Joseph in a dream.

"Joseph, son of David, do not be afraid to take Mary as your wife, for the child conceived in her is from the Holy Spirit." [Matthew 1:20]

Mary's child was conceived by the Holy Spirit.

The early Christian Church endeavored to capture this in its affirmations of faith, especially the Apostles Creed:

"I believe in God the Father Almighty, Creator of heaven and earth. I believe in Jesus Christ, his only Son, our Lord, who was conceived by the Holy Spirit, born of the Virgin Mary...."

At the point of conception, God, who is Spirit, became flesh in Jesus Christ. Jesus is the Incarnate Son of God. Incarnation means to be given form. That which is invisible is made visible; that which is abstract is made concrete; that which is Spirit is given body; that which is heavenly becomes earthly.

One of the great and profound proclamations of the Christian faith is that God chose to enter creation through the human birth process.

"The Word [of God] became flesh and lived among us, and we have seen his glory, the glory as of a father's only son, full of grace and truth." [John 1:14]

"Since the children have flesh and blood, he too shared in their humanity so that by his death he might destroy him who has the power of death.....For this purpose he had to be made like his brothers in every way, in order that he might become a merciful and faithful high priest....Because he himself suffered when he was tempted, he is able to help those who are being tempted." [Hebrews 2:14, 17, 18]

Jesus, as the Word [Logos] of God, was born in the flesh. He was truly man and in being man he experienced all that humanity experiences. Jesus was born of a woman. *"When the fullness of time had come, God sent his Son, born of a woman..."* [Galatians 4:4]

Scriptures are also careful to remind us that Jesus was fully divine. Jesus was born of the flesh. He was also born of the Spirit. Just as he bore the image of the earthly so also, he bore the image of the heavenly.

"He [Jesus] is the reflection of God's glory and the exact imprint of God's very being, and he sustains all things by his powerful word." [Hebrews 1:3]

He was born of woman [human], but he was conceived by the Holy Spirit [divine]. Just as he was fully human, he was fully divine.

Spirit gives birth to Spirit. The angel of God spoke to Joseph and said, according to the Concordant Literal Translation of the New Testament.

"Joseph, son of David, you may not be afraid to accept Miriam your wife, for that which is being generated in her is of Holy Spirit. Now she shall be bringing forth a Son, and you shall be calling His name Jesus, for He shall be saving His people from their sins." [Matthew 1:20, 21]

Jesus was born, *"not of natural descent, nor of human decision or a husband's will, but born of God."* [John 1:13 NIV] His was a physical *and* spiritual birth.

Our Physical and Spiritual Birth

We, like Jesus, are born in the flesh. We are born of a woman. The birth process must be one of the most beautiful and amazing miracles of God; it goes beyond human understanding or description.

When a child is born, he or she becomes the visible evidence of an intimate relationship that exists between the two parents. When we are born in the flesh we are born as the result of the will of man and the will of woman. We are the result of a human decision and are conceived not only in the mind of the parents, but also conceived because of their physical, sexual intercourse.

Nevertheless, the conception and development of the fetus in the womb defies definition or explanation. The Psalmist probably comes closest to describing it when saying of God,

"It was you who formed my inward parts;
you knit me together in my mother's womb.
I praise you, for I am fearfully and wonderfully made.
Wonderful are your works
that I know very well."
[Psalm 139:13, 14]

Flesh gives birth to flesh as God works the miracle of human birth from conception to delivery.

A sign in the maternity ward of a local hospital reads, "Babies are such a nice way to start people." And in the nursery unit of a local church there appears this sign that quotes I Corinthians 15:51 NIV, *"Listen, I tell you a mystery! We will not all sleep, but we will all be changed."*

All of us who share a common humanity share the common birth experience. We are all born of the flesh, conceived by the will of man and woman and the result of human decision. Scripture tells us that man and woman come together in marriage "the two shall become one flesh." In our birth, our parents do, in fact, become "one flesh."

Jesus, the Incarnate Son of God, was born in the flesh. Scriptures are careful to remind us that Jesus was fully human and identifies fully with our humanity.

They also make it clear that God desires we be clothed in the divine nature of Jesus. Just as he identifies with us in our humanity, we are called to identify with him in his divinity. We become new creatures in Christ.

"From now on, therefore, we regard no one from a human point of view, even though we once knew Christ from a human point of view, we know him no longer in that way. So, if anyone is in Christ, there is a new creation; everything old has passed away; see, everything has become new! All this is from God who reconciled us to himself through Christ..."
II Corinthians 5:16-18a

If we are to attain to the measure of the full stature of Christ, then the Holy Spirit must be allowed to bring us to spiritual birth. Jesus told Nicodemus, a Jewish teacher, that

"no one can see the kingdom of God without being born from above. No one can enter the kingdom of God without being born of water and Spirit. What is born of the flesh is flesh. What is born of the Spirit is Spirit. You must be born from above." [John 3:3, 5-7]

The Holy Spirit brings about spiritual birth. Through the working of the Holy Spirit in human life that which is born of the flesh can also experience new birth in the Spirit. It is then that we are born of the Spirit, born anew, born again, born from above, born of God. We have not only the human nature but also the divine nature within us. We become the dwelling place of God's own Spirit. [I Corinthians 3:16]

When we are born of the flesh we become the sons and daughters of our earthly parents and citizens of the kingdom of this earth. When we are born of the Spirit we become the daughters and sons of God and citizens of the Kingdom of Heaven.

"When we cry "Abba! Father!" it is that very Spirit bearing witness with our spirit that we are children of God, and if children, then heirs, heirs of God and joint heirs with Christ." [Romans 8:15b, 17a]

Because of that new birth, we are able not only to see the kingdom of God, but to enter it as a member of God's family.

One facet of the seven-fold nature of the Holy Spirit of God is to give spiritual birth to those who have been born in the flesh. As Jesus was born of the flesh and the Spirit, so it is God's plan that we be born, not only in the flesh but also the Spirit. The reason is so that we may become children of God, who is Spirit, can see and enter the eternal Kingdom of God and become co-heirs with Jesus in that Kingdom.

Jesus spoke very plainly to Nicodemus, *"You must be born from above."* The "you" is plural, meaning that all persons must be born from above, born again, born of the Spirit, if we are to be all that God has in mind for humanity – individually and collectively, to be. If I am to be what God has in mind for me to be, I, who was born in the flesh, must also be born of the Spirit.

It has been said by persons defending their lifestyle, "I was born this way." According to God's Word and Jesus' instructions, *"You must be born from above - born again."*

The Apostle Paul also spoke plainly in his letter to the Church in Rome. *"Anyone who does not have the Spirit of Christ, does not belong to him."* [Romans 8:9b] It is the Spirit who teaches us how to say *"Abba,"* acknowledging God as our heavenly parent and ourselves as God's children. Without the Spirit of Christ, we are unable to cry "Abba" and, therefore, unable to be children of God and heirs of God's Kingdom.

If we are to attain to the full measure of the stature of Christ, spiritual birth is the first step. We did not have a choice in our first birth. We did not ask to be born. However, the new birth, the spiritual birth is by decision. We ask to be born again.

Life Application

Chris, with his parents, attended a weekend spiritual renewal event that my wife and I conducted at their church. He was twelve years old. He was seated [read, *sandwiched*] between his parents for the Friday evening session, the all-day Saturday and Saturday evening sessions as well as the Sunday morning, afternoon and evening sessions. It soon became evident that Chris did not want to be there.

Following the final session on Sunday evening, the congregation gathered in the fellowship hall for refreshments and a time of visiting with each other. Chris approached me for the first time and said, "I want to talk with you, but not in here. I want to talk with you in the pastor's office."

We went into the office where Chris instructed me to sit in a chair next to the wall while he went around behind the pastor's desk and sat in a leather swivel chair. After a while he spoke with a challenging tone, "I want to talk with you about this Jesus!"

Then Chris began to unload long-buried feelings of resentment. He began with his school. He hated school. He hated the principal, the vice-principal, his teachers, his classmates, the janitor and the bus driver who drove him to school. Chris even hated recess. He expressed all his pent-up feelings about school. It took him about fifteen minutes to do so.

Chris next expressed himself about his home. He hated home. He hated his father, his mother, his siblings, his room, the chores and everything that had to do with home. That occupied another fifteen minutes.

Church was Chris's third area of resentment. He hated church. He hated the preacher, who preached the worst sermons in the world. He hated the choir, who could not sing in tune or on tempo. He hated his Sunday school teachers, his classmates and anything that had to do with church, including God. This took another fifteen minutes.

Finally, Chris expressed resentment that he harbored for himself. Chris did not like Chris. This was his major problem.

When Chris became silent, I asked, "Chris, you really want to talk about Jesus, don't you?" The Holy Spirit had reminded me that that was what Chris had said when we first came into the pastor's office, "I want to talk with you about this Jesus."

Chris responded, "Yes, I do."

I was prompted by the Spirit to ask, "Do you desire to have a relationship with Jesus? Do you want to ask Jesus into your heart?"

"Yes, I do," responded Chris.

Then I knew what God was doing in the boy's life to get him ready for this new move of the Spirit in his life. He was bringing to light and cleaning out all the bitterness, resentment and hatred so that the boy could experience new birth. I said to Chris as I moved around behind the desk where Chris was seated, "Then you will have to ask Jesus into your life yourself. I cannot do that for you."

Chris said, "Okay, I will."

Then Chris prayed like this, "God I'm sorry for the way I am. Will you forgive me?" There was a long period of silence, then he spoke, "Thank you for your forgiveness."

He continued, "Jesus, I want you to come into my heart." This was followed by another long silence. Then he said, "Thank you for coming into my heart." He continued, "Jesus, I ask you to baptize me with the Holy Spirit." Another long period of silence, then, "Thank you for baptizing me with the Holy Spirit. Amen."

Tears flowed down the boy's cheeks. Chris was born again. He was born from above. The Holy Spirit and the amazing grace of God cleansed out all the bitterness and resentments beforehand so that Chris could be open to new birth.

When Chris and I left the office, at about twelve o'clock midnight, he knew he had been born again, born from above, born of God. He was a new and different boy. He had experienced spiritual birth. He had the assurance that he was now born into the family of God.

"What is born of the flesh is flesh, and what is born of the Spirit is spirit." [John 3:6]

Personal Reflection

Take time for personal reflection on the following Scripture:

"If anyone is in Christ, he [or she] is a new creation; the old has gone, the new has come! All this is from God, who reconciled us to himself through Christ..." [II Corinthians 5:17-18a NIV]

I am a new creation. I live out this life in the flesh, but I have been born of the Spirit.

A Time to Remember

Those who have received Jesus as their Savior and Lord can remember that theirs was a step of faith that came after someone had shared with them the good news of God's Love in Christ.

The Apostle Paul reminded the Christians in Rome that before there can be a response to God they must first hear the Gospel,

"If you confess with your lips that Jesus is Lord and believe in your heart that God raised him from the dead, you will be saved." "Everyone who calls on the name of the Lord will be saved." "So, faith comes from what is heard and what is heard comes through the word of Christ." [Romans 10:9,13,17]

It is important to remember how the message of faith was spoken through persons who played an important role in our spiritual birth and nurturing process.

It is important to remember those times when the Grace of God moved in our lives to bring us into new and vital dimensions of our relationship with Jesus Christ.

It is important to recall those times that elicited faith responses on our part to the move of God's Holy Spirit. For in the remembering and the recalling, we are reminded of Gods amazing Grace as God's Spirit draws us into relationship even before we are consciously aware of it. We are also reminded of who we are as children of God.

Remember:
1. The day of my physical birth _07-10-1944_
2. Name of my parents: Father _Elwyn Glen Burt_
    Mother _Nina Thelma George Burt_
3. In what place do I remember hearing the Gospel that elicited a faith response from me? Home? Church Worship Service? Church Camp? Evangelistic Crusade? Other?

4. Who was involved in sharing the Good News of God's Love with me that brought about this response?

5. My spiritual birth day is
6. How do I know that I had a spiritual birth? Describe:

If you have not yet invited Jesus into your heart and have not asked to be born from above, this is the time. We join with the Apostle Paul in saying,

"As we work together with him, we urge you also not to accept the grace of God in vain. For he says,
> *"At an acceptable time, I have listened to you,*
> *and on a day of salvation I have helped you."*
> *See, now is the acceptable time;*
> *see, now is the day of salvation!"*

[II Corinthians 6:1,2]

SAMPLE PRAYER FOR SPIRITUAL BIRTH

"Loving and gracious God, I confess that I am a sinner. I have done those things that are not pleasing to you or helpful to me. I repent and ask you to forgive me my sin.

"Jesus, I believe that you died on the cross for my sin. I believe that in your resurrection you have provided for me the way to eternal life. I ask you to come into my heart. I receive you as the Savior of my soul and the Lord of my life.

"Jesus, fill me with your Holy Spirit. I desire to be born again. I desire to be born of your Spirit and filled with your power so that my life may become all that God has in mind for me to be.

"Thank you, gracious God, for your forgiveness. Thank you, Jesus, for coming into my heart. Thank you, Holy Spirit, for giving me new birth and a place in God's eternal Kingdom. Amen."

Spiritual birth is the first step in *"attaining to the full measure of the stature of Christ."*

CHAPTER 2

GROWING UP IN THE SPIRIT

"After eight days had passed, it was time to circumcise the child; and he was called Jesus, the name given by the angel before he was conceived in the womb." Luke 2:21,

"The child grew and became strong, filled with wisdom; and the favor of God was upon him." Luke 2:40

"Then he went down with them and came to Nazareth and was obedient to them." Luke 2:51,

Jesus' Physical and Spiritual Growth
Birth is followed by growth. While newborn babies are beautiful and a joy in the life of the parents, it is not desirable that they should stay newborn or remain as infants. Growing up is a fact of life – a desirable fact of life.

Jesus was born in a manger in Bethlehem of Judea, but he did not remain in the manger nor did he remain in Bethlehem.

The grace [Spirit] of God brings growth. The grace of God was upon Jesus throughout his formative years, enabling him to grow in knowledge, wisdom and understanding. He learned not only of the things of this world but also the things of God.

It was the custom of his parents, and so became his custom, to be in the Temple or synagogue of God on the Sabbath to offer their sacrifices and to worship the God of Abraham, Isaac and Jacob.

As devout Jews, Joseph and Mary role-modeled for their son what it means to be people of God. Even as a twelve-year-old boy, Jesus knew he had to be in God's house. [Luke 2:49] As he grew he was taught by Joseph, his father, how to work with his hands in his carpentry shop.

Jesus grew up physically, in stature, from childhood to manhood. At the same time, he grew up spiritually, in wisdom. He also grew relationally. He learned obedience. In that growth process he grew in favor with God and with those around him.

The writer of the Letter to the Hebrews reminds us that

"Since, therefore, the children share flesh and blood, he himself likewise shared the same things..."he had to become like his brothers and sisters in every respect, so that he might be a merciful and faithful high priest in the service of God....Because he himself was tested by what he suffered, he is able to help those who are being tested.". [Hebrews 2:14, 17, 18]

"We do not have a high priest who is unable to sympathize with our weaknesses, but we have one who in every respect has been tested as we are, yet without sin." [Hebrews 4:15]

Jesus was human – a growing and maturing human. He ate, slept, wept, laughed, grew tired, knew pain, faced temptation, knew success, experienced rejection, worked and did all those things that are part of being born in the flesh.

In the growth process Jesus experienced intense human emotions such as amazement, compassion, indignation, exasperation, anger and deep distress. He knew the power of love and felt the sting of loneliness and isolation as he was being rejected and crucified for his convictions.

He needed human fellowship and so developed close relationships with those who welcomed him into their homes. He had a deep love for one of the Twelve disciples, presumably John, but he loved the others as well. He loved Lazarus as a brother and wept over his death.

He knew how to accept intimate expressions of love as a woman's tears fell on his feet and she dried them with her hair. Another poured expensive oils and fragrant perfumes on his head.

Jesus experienced humanity's spiritual, emotional, physical and relational state completely. He shared in humanity's humanness with one exception, he did not sin.

As Jesus grew physically, emotionally and relationally, he also grew spiritually. The Spirit of God developed within Jesus those qualities that reflected the very nature of God. He knew the love of God. He experienced the joy and peace of God. He came to understand the patience, kindness and goodness of God. He experienced the faithfulness, gentleness and self-control of God. The fruit of God's Spirit grew in his life.

We may assume that the first thirty years of Jesus' life – years that are often called 'the hidden years,' were spent in growing. Growth implies maturing. To grow is to have a teachable spirit and a desire to be taught and to learn. Growth produces change.

Whatever else may have happened in those thirty or so years since his birth, of this one thing we can be sure, the baby born in Bethlehem is now a mature man, fully changed, fully aware of who he is and fully committed to be that which he was called by God to be. Jesus grew in wisdom and stature and in favor with God and people.

Our Physical and Spiritual Growth

Physical birth is followed by physical growth. In our own maturation process, we experience all those things that make us human. We learn to imitate the sounds others are making, to learn a language. We learn and follow the moral, social and ethical codes of the culture in which we find ourselves.

We are surrounded by adult role-models who set examples – some positive and some less than positive, for us to follow. We are faced with decisions as to which example we will choose to follow. We learn that we have a free will and must assume responsibility for the choices we make.

We experience human weakness, temptations of the flesh, rejections, hurts, traumas and "growing pains." We also experience support, encouragement, honor, praise and "feeling good" times. Our growing up is a mixture of experiences that shape us into the persons we are.

Hopefully, during this physical growth period we are also growing in knowledge, wisdom and understanding as well. It is not appropriate for an adult body to house a brain that has failed to mature beyond the infant level. When Jesus said that unless we become like children we will never see the Kingdom of God, he was talking about being child<u>like</u>, not child<u>ish</u>.

Childlikeness is very desirable in an adult. Childishness is extremely unproductive and, in fact, has no place in the Christian life or in the Kingdom of God. Childishness is immaturity at whatever age level.

Physical growth implies growth in other areas. It implies developing into mature adults in our emotions and in our relations with other people. It implies learning obedience and the meaning of commitment. It implies learning how to make just decisions and to exhibit socially acceptable behavior.

Physical growth is a fact of life and carries with it the responsibility to learn how to be an adult. Though living in an imperfect world, we must learn to be able to distinguish between that behavior that is counter-productive – and even destructive, and that which brings our life to the level of productivity that unveils the potential that is wrapped up in the human person. Physical birth is naturally followed by physical growth.

In the same way, spiritual birth is followed by spiritual growth. Justification is followed by sanctification. Following our spiritual birth, the Holy Spirit works to "grow us up" spiritually. The Holy Spirit works to cleanse and make ready our lives for Kingdom living. Once we are born into the Kingdom of God, we begin to learn Kingdom living through the work of the indwelling Holy Spirit. Jesus is our Role-model. The Holy Spirit is our Teacher.

Growth implies change from one level of maturity to another. Through the work of the Holy Spirit we are being changed more and more into the likeness of Jesus, the one image that God has in mind for all.

"And all of us, with unveiled faces.... are being transformed into the same image from one degree of glory to another; for this comes from the Lord, the Spirit." [II Corinthians 3:18]

In our formative spiritual years, the Holy Spirit "grows us up" in wisdom and understanding, not only of the things of this world, but also the things of God. We learn that as we live by the Spirit we will not gratify the desires of the sinful, fleshly nature.

We learn that the fleshly nature desires what is contrary to the Spirit and the spiritual nature desires what is contrary to the sinful nature. They conflict with each other. [Galatians 5:17] The Holy Spirit teaches us how to distinguish between the two.

Spiritual growth comes as the fruit of the Spirit matures in our lives. It is during this time that we experience the growing presence of love, a quality of love that begins to show up with joy, peace, patience, kindness, goodness, faithfulness, gentleness and self-control.

All these spiritual qualities, that reflect the very nature of God, were evident in the life of Jesus. And so, in our lives spiritual growth and maturity become realities as the fruit of the Spirit is developed in us.

Whatever else may happen in these formative years, one thing is for certain, we must be open to spiritual growth as well as physical growth if we are to experience the Holy Spirit accomplishing in our lives what was accomplished in the life of Jesus.

Spiritual growth is a life-long process. It involves every facet of our lives – spirit, soul [mind, will and emotions], body and relationships. It involves our whole being. In whatever way the Spirit of God may be working in our lives, growth is involved in that process.

We learn obedience to God just as Jesus learned obedience.

"I do what the Father has commanded me, so that the world may know that I love the Father." [John 14:31]

We learn discipline as Jesus learned it.

"The Lord disciplines those whom he loves and chastises every child whom he accepts. Endure trials for the sake of discipline. God is treating you as children, for what child is there whom a parent does not discipline?" [Hebrews 12:6, 7]

We learn how to worship, to pray and to study the Scriptures just as Jesus learned these holy habits. We learn how to make sacrifices just as he sacrificed. We learn compassion as he learned it. We learn how to serve and to have a servant's heart just as Jesus learned it and taught it to his disciples. [Mark 9:33-37]

That which the Holy Spirit worked in the life of Jesus as he grew in wisdom and stature, the Spirit also works in our lives, bringing us into that image that God has for us and which has been revealed in the life of Jesus.

Mature Christians reflect the spiritual fruit that is *seen* in the life of Jesus. Mature Christians reflect the spiritual maturity that is *demonstrated* in the life of Jesus. Mature Christians are those who "grow up' into him who is the Head, that is Christ, and become the Body of Christ, the Church.

They are no longer spiritual infants, *"tossed to and fro and blown about by every wind of doctrine, by people's trickery, by their craftiness in deceitful scheming. But speaking the truth in love, we must grow up in every way into him who is the head, into Christ."* [Ephesians 4:14, 15]

Maturing Christians develop a childlike faith that is teachable and trusting, and an adult-like desire and willingness to be made over into the image of Jesus.

John Wesley, the great eighteenth century spiritual leader, reformer and founder of the Methodist movement, preached a sermon on "The New Birth." In that sermon he said,

"When we are born again, then our sanctification, our inward and outward holiness, begins; and thence forward we are gradually to 'grow up' in him who is our head. This expression admirably illustrates the difference between one and the other, and farther points out the exact analogy there is between natural and spiritual things.

"A child is born of a woman in a moment, or at least in a very short time. Afterwards he gradually and slowly grows until he attains to the full stature of a man. In like manner a child is born of God in a short time, if not in a moment. But it is by slow degrees that he afterwards grows up to the measure of the full stature of Christ.

"The same relations therefore which there is between our natural birth and our growth, there is also between our new birth and our sanctification." [end quote]

Spiritual growth follows spiritual birth.

Life Application

Pastor John moved to the desert of Southern California where he became minister to some of the people called "snowbirds" who traveled south for the winter to escape the cold in the northern tier states in the United States. I had made a "pastoral call" on some of my "snowbird" parishioners who had travelled south for the winter.

On Sunday we attended Pastor John's services together. During one of his Sunday services he told the story of his own move to the desert. His new place of residence was surrounded by deciduous trees that lost their leaves when summer turned to fall and winter.

He noticed that one of the trees retained its leaves, though they were dead and brown. The desert storms carrying wind, rain and snow, did not strip the leaves that hung tenaciously to the limbs of the tree. They remained on the tree throughout the winter months.

As spring approached, he noticed that all the other trees that were bare through the winter were getting their coats of new green leaves. The one tree only now began to lose its brown leaves. He thought that it was diseased and had considered having it cut down. However, as he examined it he discovered the reason for the old leaves just now falling. As the new green shoots were developing, they pushed off the old, dead leaves one at a time. This tree had an entirely different growth pattern from the others.

As he shared that story about the tree, the Holy Spirit spoke to my heart. I had been wrestling with some old habits and thought patterns that hung tenaciously to my life. Try as I would I could not rid myself of thoughts that had been destructive to me and to relationships that I had with others - especially in my family. I discovered that I was powerless on my own to *"take every thought captive,"* as instructed in Scripture. [II Corinthians 10:5]

I was discouraged about my inability, as a Christian - and a pastor, to overcome some old ways. I had not yet learned that when the old ways and thoughts show up they simply remind me of the way I used to be, not the way I am now. That had not yet become a part of my understanding of what it means to be a new creation in Christ.

However, the Spirit of God witnessed to my inner self and told me that if I would focus on developing a close and good relationship with God, the Holy Spirit would take care of the old ways. If I would allow the Spirit to work in my life, the new growth would push off the old habits and thought patterns. I was to put my mind and heart on "things above."

I began to take my mind off my old, sinful and destructive habits and focus, instead, on the life-transforming work of God and the possibilities of what God could do with my life. As a result, in time the old ways began to fall away as the Spirit crowded them out with a new way of living and thinking. The Holy Spirit replaced the old with the new.

Our spiritual birth is, of necessity, followed by our spiritual growth. It is in this period of our spiritual development that we grow in grace and, under the enabling work of the Holy Spirit, put aside the fleshly nature, the sinful nature and take on the nature of God in our lives. The fruit of the Spirit becomes evident as the Love of God is made visible in us.

Personal Reflection

Think about this Scripture as you apply it to your own life:

"And all of us [including me] *with unveiled faces, seeing the glory of the Lord as though reflected in a mirror, are* [I am] *being transformed into the same image from one degree of glory to another; for this comes from the Lord, the Spirit."* [II Corinthians 3:18]

Do I see myself as a person being transformed, changed, into Jesus' likeness?

What does this Scripture tell you about God's plan for your life?

"From now on, therefore, we regard no one from a human point of view; even though we once knew Christ from a human point of view, we know him no longer in that way. So, if anyone is in Christ, there is a new creation: everything old has passed away; see, everything has become new!" [II Corinthians 5:16, 17]

A Time to Remember

Remember those physical, emotional and relational growth experiences that had profound effect upon your life. What were those "transforming" experiences that brought change?

1. The most positive experiences in my "growing up" years were:

   _____
   _____
   _____
   _____

2. Growth is not always easy. These are the areas of my life that I found to be very difficult in growing up. These are the "brown leaf" areas.

   _____
   _____
   _____
   _____

3. Date of my baptism_____
4. Date of my graduation_____
5. Date of my wedding [if applicable] _____
   My Spouses name is_____
6. I became a member of the_____Church on_____, _____.
7. These are the holy habits that I am developing in my life as I grow in my faith:
   a. Worship
   b. Study of Scripture
   c. Prayer
   d. Serving
   e. Giving
   f. Other
8. I have found the following Fruit of the Holy Spirit to be evident in my life: Galatians 5:22

   _____
   _____
   _____

9. I have found the following Fruit of the Holy Spirit has a more difficult time growing in my life:

   _____
   _____

10. People and circumstances that are helping me to mature in:
    Wisdom _____
    Understanding _____
    Obedience _____
    Discipline _____
    My Discipleship _____
    Service _____
11. I desire to be more Christ-like in my _____
    _____

12. These are the persons who have provided support and encouragement to me as I have grown in my faith:
    Parents: _____
    Grandparents: _____
    Teachers: _____
    Other significant individuals: _____

PRAYER: "Loving and gracious God, I pray that by the power of your Holy Spirit you will help me grow up in my life and faith and into the image you have for me. As I grow in stature, may I also grow in wisdom, obedience and in favor with You and the people around me.

Holy Spirit, I give you permission to work God's perfect will in my life and develop your spiritual fruit in me so that I may grow up to be like Jesus, in whose Name I pray. Amen"

CHAPTER 3

BAPTIZED WITH THE SPIRIT

"Now when all the people were baptized, and when Jesus also had been baptized and was praying, the heaven was opened, and the Holy Spirit descended upon him in bodily form like a dove. And a voice came from heaven, "You are my Son, the Beloved; with you I am well pleased." Luke 3:21, 22

Jesus' Physical and Spirit Baptism

Jesus was conceived by the Holy Spirit and born of the Holy Spirit. He grew up under the counsel and guidance of the Holy Spirit. Then his life was impacted in a new and powerful way by the Holy Spirit at the time of his baptism.

Jesus was about thirty years of age when he was baptized in the River Jordan by John the Baptizer, as he was known.

Circumcision was the sign of the covenant between God and the Jewish people. It was a Covenant established by God with Abraham and his descendants. Through this Covenant the people of Israel were known as the children of Abraham and so each child was circumcised on the eighth day after birth and identified with and in the family of Abraham.

Gentile converts to Judaism, however, were, in addition to circumcision, required to be baptized as a sign of cleansing and preparation for inclusion in the Covenant community of faith.

John the Baptizer, an acknowledged prophet – and the first for over four hundred years, came preaching a baptism of repentance not only for the Gentiles but for the Jewish believers as well. He preached *"a baptism of repentance for the forgiveness of sins."* [Mark 1:4]

Always before, the prophets had preached of the coming Kingdom of God in the future, but now John is preaching that the Kingdom is "at hand," and cleansing is essential for all people, Jew and Gentile alike, to be prepared.

When Jesus came to be baptized in water, John protested that it was he who should be baptized by Jesus. Nevertheless, Jesus insisted that it be done. *"Let it be so now, for it is proper for us in this way to fulfill all righteousness."* [Matthew 3:15] John baptized Jesus.

Jesus, in his humanity, is identifying with the fallen state of all humanity, Jew and Gentile alike. It is true that he took on the sins of humanity as he went to the cross, but he publicly identified with sinful humanity as he walked into the Jordan River for John to baptize him. John's was a baptism for repentance and Jesus accepted that baptism though he had done nothing for which he needed to repent and from which he needed to be cleansed.

Could he have been repenting for the sins of all humanity in that act? Precedent had already been set for this act of repentance for the sins of others. When Israel was in exile in Babylonia, in the early 7th century B.C. Daniel, prophet of Israel and a young member of Jewish nobility, was among them.

During that time, Daniel, in his obedience to God, repented of Israel's sins in which he had not participated, yet with which he identified and claimed as his own. He was part of the community and identified with it. [Daniel 9:4-19]

Likewise, each year the High Priest of the Jewish Faith entered the Holy of Holies in the Temple in Jerusalem to confess Israel's sin and to intercede for the people. As High Priest, he identified with all the sins of all the people though he may not have participated in them himself. He interceded on behalf of all Israel, including himself. He was part of the community of faith and so identified with it.

In the same manner, Jesus humbled himself, identified himself with sinful humanity, repented on behalf of all for humanity's sin, walked into the Jordan River and was baptized by John *"for righteousness sake."*

At the time of his baptism in the waters of the Jordan River, there was a new move of the Holy Spirit upon his life. He was baptized with water, but he was also baptized with the Holy Spirit for, as the Scriptures record, the Holy Spirit "descended on him."

Though he was born of the Spirit and grew up in the Spirit, he now has a new encounter with the Holy Spirit unlike the previous ones. He was baptized with the Holy Spirit. As he was coming up out of the water, *"he saw the heavens torn apart and the Spirit descending like a dove on him."* [Mark 1:9-11; Matthew 3:13-17; Luke 3:21, 22]

It is interesting to note that the Spirit came as a dove and not as a lamb. Jesus was certainly identified by John the Baptizer as *"the Lamb of God who takes away the sins of the world."* [John 1:29] Jesus was the Lamb of God. However, in each of the Gospel baptism accounts, the Holy Spirit of God comes upon Jesus in the form of a dove.

In the Levitical Law, the dove is the poor peoples' sacrifice. [Leviticus 5:7] Jesus became, in fact, the poor peoples' sacrifice through his death on the cross to take away humanity's sin.

Jesus was immersed in the love of God from his birth. As he grew up, he grew in wisdom as well as stature. He grew in favor with God and with people around him. He learned of the love of God during those years he spent in synagogue school memorizing Holy Scripture. He learned to feast on the word of God and know that it was sweeter than honey from the honeycomb.

One tradition states that the teacher or rabbi, at the opening of the school year, would cover the student's slate with honey and have the students lick their slate clean before writing on it. This was done to remind the students that God's Word is sweet as honey from the honeycomb. [Psalm 19:10; 119:103] Jesus knew of God's love for him. Even at the age of twelve he had a deep sense of need to be in God's house, in God's presence and among God's chosen spiritual leaders. [Luke 2:41ff]

At his baptism in the Jordan River he heard the voice of God, his heavenly Father say, *"You are my son, the Beloved; with you I am well pleased."* [Luke 3:22]

When the Holy Spirit came upon him at his baptism, the direction for his ministry was set. Jesus was baptized in water. He was also baptized with the Holy Spirit and the direction for his earthly ministry was set.

From the beginning Jesus set out to be obedient to God's call on his life and to follow the lead of God's Holy Spirit. Love became the motivating force and core value behind his life and ministry. His great command to his disciples was that they love one another as he had loved them.

This quality of love demonstrated among them would also be the visible evidence to everyone that they were truly his disciples. *"By this everyone will know that you are my disciples, if you have love for one another."* [John 13 35]

Jesus, the Son of God, was baptized in water by John the baptizer at which time he identified with sinful humanity. At the same time, the Holy Spirit came upon Jesus, the Son of Man, and baptized him with the eternal, powerful and God-announced Love that the Father has for the son.

Our own spiritual journey begins as the Holy Spirit brings us to new birth. It is by God's grace and the wooing of God's Spirit that we are enabled to say "Yes" to Jesus as our Savior and Lord.

Then the Holy Spirit "grows us up" more and more into the image of Jesus Christ and enables us to truly have the mind of Christ, [I Corinthians 2:16] learning to think as he thinks, to will what he wills and to do what he does.

Our Physical and Spirit Baptism

Baptism is an integral part of our Christian life. We are baptized in water as we are incorporated into the Body of Christ and into the family of God. In water baptism we identify with the old, sinful nature, claiming it as our own, repenting of it and expressing a willingness to let the old nature die and be washed away. We are baptized "for righteousness' sake."

In that same act we come up out of the water and claim resurrection from that death. In water baptism the old, sinful nature is buried and the new creation is raised from the grave. [Colossians 2:12] The old is gone, the new has come.

Tradition has it that early church baptism took place in running water, usually the Jordan River. Persons would wade into the water in their old clothes. At the time of their baptism the old clothes would be removed and allowed to float down the river, symbolizing that the old life was washed away.

The candidates were then baptized naked, as a sign of dying to self. A clean white robe was placed around them as they came up out of the water, symbolizing the fact that they were raised to new life in Christ Jesus.

The beautiful imagery captured by this act is still very much a part of the life of the Church. In baptism we are buried with Christ, our sins are washed away, and we are raised to new life with him in his resurrection.

There is another baptism. It is baptism with the Holy Spirit. John the Baptizer told the people who came out to him to be baptized,

"I baptize you with water, but one who is more powerful than I is coming. He will baptize you with the Holy Spirit and fire." [Luke 3:16]

Jesus told his disciples,

"John baptized with water, but you will be baptized with the Holy Spirit not many days from now." [Acts 1:5]

Jesus had been teaching the disciples about the promised Holy Spirit and so he instructed them to wait in Jerusalem for the Holy Spirit. On Pentecost they received what Jesus had promised, the Holy Spirit was poured out on them.

Like Jesus, we are baptized with water. In our baptism we are incorporated into the Body of Christ, the Church. Likewise, as with Jesus, we are also baptized with the Holy Spirit and with fire. This baptism immerses us in the Spirit and nature of God and into God's eternal and life-transforming love. It also empowers us to be about the ministry to which God has called us. [Acts 1:8]

The Holy Spirit came upon Jesus in bodily form like a dove. The Holy Spirit did not come upon the one hundred and twenty disciples at Pentecost in the form of a dove, but rather as tongues of fire that divided and rested upon each of them. That Holy Spirit baptism experience set the direction for their ministry as they were to proclaim the Good News in the languages of men and angels.

The Holy Spirit came upon the twelve Disciples in the Upper Room as Breath from God, as Jesus breathed on them and said, *"Receive the Holy Spirit."* [John 20:21-23]

Baptism with the Holy Spirit empowers the people of God for ministry. To be baptized with or in the Holy Spirit is to experience the outpouring of God's own Person upon our lives to the point where we become the dwelling place of God's own Spirit.

Jesus heard God say, *"This is my Son; the Beloved, with whom I am well pleased,"* even as the Holy Spirit descended upon him. It is the same Holy Spirit who enables us to cry, *"Abba! Father!"* and also enables us to know God's love that surpasses knowledge. It is the time at which we hear the voice of God say, and the Spirit of God gives witness to our spirit, "You are my child, my beloved. With you I am well pleased." Love becomes the motivating force in our lives and ministries.

When the Holy Spirit "comes upon" us, the direction for our lives and ministry is set. It involves witnessing, obedience, servant-hood, sacrifice and a heart for the poor. It involves giving testimony to the working of God in our lives and witnessing to the grace of God in Christ for all humanity

The Holy Spirit comes upon God's people in ways that set the direction for the work that they are called to do. The Holy Spirit will be manifested differently in each life but working the same miracles of grace through every life.

The Apostle Paul stated that,

"Now there are varieties of gifts, but the same Spirit; and there are varieties of services, but the same Lord; and there are varieties of activities, but it is the same God who activates all of them in everyone." [I Corinthians 12:4-6]

Baptize means to immerse, to submerge, to be overwhelmed with that in which we are immersed. The word also means "to dye," as in changing the color of a garment.

Both meanings are clear in the life of a person who is baptized with the Holy Spirit. They are immersed in the eternal nature and love of God. They are submerged in the God who is Holy [Leviticus 11:44], in the God who is Spirit [John 4:24], in the God who is Consuming Fire [Hebrews 12:29], in the God who is Light [I John 1:5] and in the God who is Love [I John 4:16]. In the process, their lives are changed into Jesus' likeness *"with ever-increasing glory."* [2 Corinthians 3:18]

This baptism is the total immersion of our whole person – spirit, soul [mind, will, emotions] and body, in the eternal nature of the living God. It is the time when we are overwhelmed by God's Love. Each person may experience that love in a different way even as different children in the same family experience and respond to their parent's love in different ways. Nevertheless, the Love is poured out equally on each one and all alike.

The Apostle Paul asked some disciples in Ephesus,

"Did you receive the Holy Spirit when you became believers?" They replied, "No, we have not even heard that there is a Holy Spirit.," Then he said, "Into what were you baptized?" They answered, "Into John's baptism." Paul said, "John baptized with the baptism of repentance, telling the people to believe in the one who was to come after him, that is, in Jesus." On hearing this, they were baptized in the name of the Lord Jesus. When Paul had laid his hands on them, the Holy Spirit came upon them...." [Acts 19:1-7]

John's baptism was a baptism of repentance and forgiveness. The Holy Spirit's baptism is a baptism for transformation and empowerment. Jesus told his disciples, *"You will receive power when the Holy Spirit has come upon you and you will be my witnesses."* Acts 1:8

The Holy Spirit may impact a person's life like "ruach" or "pneuma," like breath or wind. The Spirit's presence may be as silent as a breath or whisper and subtle as a sunrise. That presence may also be as powerfully forceful as hurricane wind and as visible as a forest fire. Whichever way the Spirit may choose to move on people's lives, there will be the inner witness and knowing that we are children of God, accepted by God, loved by God and loved with a love from which nothing will ever be able to separate us.

As the apostle Paul said in his letter to the Christians in Rome,
"I am convinced that neither death, nor life, nor angels, nor rulers, nor things present, nor things to come, nor powers, nor height, nor depth, nor anything else in all creation, will be able to separate us from the love of God in Christ Jesus our Lord." [Romans 8:38, 39]

This encounter with the Holy Spirit, and the overwhelming love of God, sets the direction for the rest of our lives and ministry – as it did with Jesus.

What Jesus did at the cross had its beginning in the River Jordan when the Spirit came upon him in the form of a dove.

What the disciples did in Jerusalem, Judea, Samaria, Greece and Italy had its beginning in the Upper Room when the Holy Spirit came upon them with tongues of fire.

The direction for what you and I do as disciples of Jesus and ministers of the Gospel of God has its beginning in that moment when the Holy Spirit comes upon us and baptizes us in the life-transforming and life-empowering Love of God. It puts in our hearts a passion for the gospel of Christ and a burning desire to share it with others.

Jesus told the disciples to wait in Jerusalem until they received the gift that God had promised, which they had heard him speak about. He reminded them that John baptized with water but, in a few days, they would be baptized with the Holy Spirit and with fire. It happened on the day of Pentecost. God's promised Gift of the Holy Spirit came upon the disciples, as Jesus had said it would.

Jesus also told them that they would receive power when the Holy Spirit came upon them and then they would be his witnesses. [Acts 1:8] This was not an optional encounter it was a basic requirement if they, who live, walked and talked with Jesus, were to experience the supernatural power that they needed to do the supernatural ministry to which God assigned them.

Baptism with the Holy Spirit is not optional for us any more than it was for Jesus or the early disciples. If we are to grow up and come to full maturity in Jesus Christ, the Holy Spirit of God must have the freedom to work that work in our lives that empowers us to live out that life and ministry that God assigns to us. Human effort alone is insufficient.

Life Application

After eighteen years of pastoral ministry I experienced burnout. I was physically, emotionally, relationally and spiritually spent. That on which I once thrived, I no longer enjoyed. I had lost my zeal for preaching, teaching and praying. For those whom I once cared, I now found I had little or no interest. I was physically weary, emotionally drained and spiritually anemic.

While still in high school I believed that I had received a call from God to enter pastoral ministry. My decisions relative to education, family and future were predicated on that belief.

My wife and I were married shortly after graduating from high school and, together, we began the process of preparation for pastoral ministry. While a sophomore in college I was asked to be a Student Lay Pastor of a small, metropolitan church, at which I served until graduation. Our two children were born while we were serving that church.

This was followed by three years of seminary and assignment to another student pastorate during that time. The years were difficult. I was endeavoring to learn how to be a husband and father while, at the same time, learning how to be a pastor and complete my education. Yet, at the same time, the years were full of excitement and anticipation for what was in store for us in the future.

Following graduation from seminary I found myself engaged in "full time" ministry and assigned to a small church in a rural farming community.

The next twelve years were spent in good churches that experienced growth under my leadership. There was an increase in attendance and participation in worship and other church activities. Youth groups grew, and budgets grew also. And, for me, ever-increasing leadership roles in our denominational structure came along with the evident success in the local churches. It appeared that I would have a very "successful" ministry, based on the presupposition that larger churches and larger salaries are to be equated with "success."

However, in my twelfth year and third church after graduation from seminary, I experienced physical, emotional and spiritual burn-out. I could not understand the cause at the time.

Later, as I looked back on it, I realized that it came largely from an attitude that I had acquired during the years of my academic preparation for ministry: "If I want it done correctly, I will have to do it myself."

This was only reinforced by a work ethic that had been developed while growing up in a migrant worker family where productivity determined the amount of the income received.

During my seminary training I remember being taught that I could not expect the laity to do the work of ministry that I was called to do. Therefore, I interpreted that as meaning that they were not to do ministry or, most certainly only limited ministry. "Don't expect other people to do your work. Do it yourself."

The denomination in which I serve was originally grounded in a radical commitment to Jesus Christ and a firm belief in the priesthood of all believers. The laity, not the ordained clergy, were the ones who did ministry. It was the task of the ordained clergy to *"equip the saints for the work of ministry."* [Ephesians 4:12]

At some point in time the emphasis began to be placed on the ordained clergyperson as the one being in ministry. I had evidently taken that so seriously that I burned out in the process of trying to do it all myself.

During that period of burn-out, my superiors, who were not aware of my emotional state, called and asked if I would be willing to assume pastoral leadership of another church. I reasoned that since it was a larger church with a larger budget and salary, and – not so co-incidentally, closer to the denominational offices, it would probably be a good career move. Perhaps the new start would restore some of my former enthusiasm for ministry.

The time for the new assignment came, but not before my superiors told me about persons in that church who were baptized with the Holy Spirit and some of whom spoke in tongues. "Can you handle that?" they asked.

I responded by saying, "Sure, I can handle that. What is it?"

I had always had a belief in God, I knew God. At least, I knew about God. Since my conversion at the age of sixteen I had known Jesus as my Savior and Lord and, like those who had gone before me in ministry, I "preached Christ." However, for some reason, I had not come to know the Third Person of the Triune Godhead, the Holy Spirit.

In all my reading of the Scriptures my eyes, mind and understanding had been closed to the many passages that spoke of the Person and Work of the Holy Spirit. I could not remember having had any teaching on the Holy Spirit while in seminary. If, indeed there was teaching about the Holy Spirit, my ears were closed to hearing it.

I had no real understanding of the Holy Spirit or of any of the spiritual gifts, including speaking in tongues – except I knew that "that" church in another part of town did "things like that." But I never took time to inquire about "things like that."

I moved to my new appointment and, along with all my other pastoral duties, endeavored to make myself aware of those about whom I had been informed.

What I discovered was a group of committed, dedicated and loving disciples who enjoyed being in ministry. They taught, visited the sick, prayed and gave liberally of themselves and their resources for the sake of Christ and his church. They appeared to be what Scripture had described as the Church, the Body of Christ.

It did not take long for me to realize that they had something in their lives that I did not have in mine. They had a love, a joy, a peace, a power that was unknown in me. And, they were not burned out!

At first, I felt threatened by this. As they told me that they were praying for me, I interpreted that to mean that they were praying that I would be the kind of pastor they wanted me to be. It seemed that I had spent my professional life endeavoring to live up to some image and expectation placed on me by others. I simply was not going to allow that to happen again. And so, I resisted.

However, as they continued in their love and prayer support, it soon became evident that they were not praying for me to be what they wanted me to be. They were praying that I would become all that God had in mind for me to become.

Soon I began to desire to have in my life what they had in theirs. After about six months – and on the day of Epiphany, that day on which the Wise Men brought their gifts to the Christ child, God's promised Gift was poured out upon my life. I was baptized with the Holy Spirit. I was totally immersed in the Love of God. I was summarily healed of my burn-out and restored to physical, emotional, relational and spiritual wholeness. It was like being brought from darkness to light, from fragmentation to wholeness, from dumb to smart, from death to life!

It was at that time I heard the voice of God say, audibly, "You have been telling people for eighteen years that I love them, and I do. But I want you to know that I love you too." That changed my life and it changed the direction of my ministry. No longer was I a "do-it-yourself" pastor. I knew I was in co-ministry with Jesus and with my brothers and sisters in Christ.

My prayers were to have in my heart and life that desire that was in the heart and life of Jesus who *"came down from heaven not to do my own will but the will of the One who sent me."* [John 6:38] And, to do that will, not under my own power, but in the power of God's Holy Spirit.

The next thirteen years of ministry were spent in that local church where, along with the laity, I grew in the Spirit, attaining to a fuller measure of the fullness of Christ in my life through the work of the Holy Spirit.

Since that time, I, with my wife - at the time of this writing, have spent another thirty years in ministry beyond the local church in the field of evangelism, *"equipping the saints for works of ministry."* There has been no further burnout, but only the continuing joy of ministering in the power of the Holy Spirit.

When we are baptized with the Holy Spirit, as was Jesus, and when we are baptized with the fire of the Spirit, as were the disciples, then we experience a supernatural presence in our lives that enables us to minister far beyond our natural, human capabilities.

If we are to follow the example of Jesus and if we are to be empowered to be effective and productive witnesses for Jesus Christ, then, as with the early disciples, we must allow the Holy Spirit to empower us. That power comes only through allowing Jesus to baptize us with His Holy Spirit.

Personal Reflection

Take time for personal reflection on the following Scriptures:

"Out of the believer's heart shall flow rivers of living water. Now he said this about the Spirit, which believers in him were to receive." [John 7:38,39a]

"John baptized with water but you will be baptized with the Holy Spirit not many days from now." [Acts 1:5]

Seeking Prayer for those who have not yet experienced being baptized with the Holy Spirit but who desire to receive that which Jesus promised to those who follow him:

"O God, you are faithful and true to your Word. You have said in your Word that you would give your Holy Spirit to those who ask. I desire to be like your Son, Jesus, and have your Spirit work in my life as in his.

I ask you to baptize me with your Holy Spirit. Fill me with your eternal love and power so that I may be yours in spirit, soul and body. Empower me to be about the ministry to which you have called me.

Thank you for baptizing me with your Holy Spirit according to your Word. Amen" [Luke 11:13]

Prayer of Thanksgiving for those who have experienced being Baptized with the Holy Spirit: "O God, you have kept your Word and baptized me with your Holy Spirit. You have immersed me in your eternal love and enabled me to walk in the way that leads to Life. I give thanks to you for the gift of your Holy Spirit and for my life being the temple in which you have chosen to reside. Let me always be aware of your Presence and give thanks for your greatness. In the Name of Christ my Lord, I pray. Amen"

A Time to Remember

In our spiritual growth it is important to remember how the Holy Spirit has worked in our lives. Remember

1. The day on which you were baptized with the Holy Spirit. [Remember that this could have been on the same day you were baptized with water or it could have been a separate time: _____. Perhaps today_____.

2. Describe that time when you were baptized with the Holy Spirit._____
   _____
   _____
   _____
   _____
   _____

3. Who was instrumental in helping you understand the need to be baptized with the Holy Spirit?

4. What do you sense to be the direction for the ministry for which you have been empowered by the Holy Spirit to do? _____
   _____

CHAPTER 4

LED AND TESTED BY THE SPIRIT

"Then Jesus was led up by the Spirit into the wilderness to be tempted by the devil. He fasted forty days and forty nights, and afterwards he was famished. The tempter came and said to him, "If you are the Son of God, command these stones to become loaves of bread." But he answered, "it is written,

"One does not live by bread alone,
but by every word that comes from the mouth of God."'

Then the devil took him to the holy city and placed him on the pinnacle of the temple, saying to him, "If you are the Son of God, throw yourself down; for it is written,

'He will command his angels concerning you.' and
'On their hands they will bear you up,
so that you will not dash your foot against a stone.'"

Jesus said to him, "Again it is written,

'Do not put the Lord you God to the test.'"

Again, the devil took him to a very high mountain and showed him all the kingdoms of the world and their splendor, and he said to him, "All these I will give you, if you will fall down and worship me." Jesus said to him, "Away with you, Satan! for it is written,

'Worship the Lord your God,
and serve only him.'"

Then the devil left him, and suddenly angels came and waited on him.

[Matthew 4:1-10]

The Gospel writer, Luke, also states that

"Jesus, full of the Holy Spirit, returned from the Jordan and was led by the Spirit into the desert where for forty days he was tempted by the devil."

[Luke 4:1 NIV]

Following the powerful encounter with the Spirit of God at the Jordan River, Jesus had a powerful encounter with the Adversary in the wilderness.

While in the wilderness, Jesus fasted and prayed for forty days and nights. He was tempted by Satan to perform various miracles that would, in fact, show him to be who he claimed to be. If he were truly the Son of God, then he should be able to validate that claim with miracles.

Led by the Spirit and the word of God, Jesus countered each temptation by focusing squarely upon the trustworthiness of God's Word.

The First Temptation: The first temptation had to do with satisfying personal needs, and, perhaps on a nobler level, miraculously satisfying the needs of hungry humanity.

After fasting for forty days and nights Jesus was hungry. However, the issue was not hunger or feeding hungry humanity.

The adversary tempted him to prove himself to be the Son of God. *"If you are the Son of God,"* said the tempter *"command this stone to become loaves of bread."* [Matthew 4:3] If you truly are who you say you are, then prove it.

The **temptation** had to do with turning stone to bread. The **issue,** however, was whether Jesus is God's Son. In fact, the issue has to do with doubt, pride and self. The **truth** is, Jesus **is** the Son of God!

"If you are," could create doubt and cause questioning as to whether Jesus is truly the Son of God. And too, being "the Son of God," could be a source of pride, for as the Son of God, Jesus could do just about anything He desired to do. Turning stone into bread, of course, would show himself not only to be who He said He was, but would demonstrate to the Adversary – and thus to the world, his miraculous powers. In the process his own basic human need for food would be met.

The **temptation** was to work a miracle. The **issue** was Jesus' Son-ship. Jesus resisted the temptation to work a miracle to prove his Son-ship. He did not have to prove his Son-ship. It was a given fact!

Jesus faced the issue by relying upon the Word of God that He had learned during his years of being in the synagogue and Temple. He drew upon that Word and submitted himself to it as his way of resisting temptation.

*"It is written, 'One does not live by bread alone,
but by every word that comes from the mouth of God.'"* Matthew.4:4

For Jesus, the issue is not bread but faith in God's Word. Jesus had heard the audible word of God spoken at his baptism, *"This is my son, the beloved, with whom I am well pleased."* He believed that word.

In later years, James, the brother of Jesus, wrote, *"Submit yourselves, therefore, to God. Resist the devil and he will flee from you."* [James 4:7] James had probably seen this demonstrated in the life of his older brother, for in confrontation with the Adversary, Jesus submitted himself to God which empowered him to resist the devil.

During his formative years Jesus had already been learning and practicing submitting himself to God. This did not begin with his baptism in the Jordan River. Jesus drew on the Word that had been planted in his heart during his younger years.

"The devil said to him, "If you are the son of God, command this stone to become loaves of bread." Jesus answered him, "It is written, 'One does not live on bread alone.'"

The Second Temptation: The Adversary also knows Scripture and is obviously a literalist. The second temptation, according to the Gospel writer Matthew [4:5, 6], is for Jesus to throw himself from the highest point of the temple.

"Then the devil took him to the holy city, and placed him on the pinnacle of the temple, saying to him, "If you are the Son of God, throw yourself down from here, for it is written,
'He will command his angels concerning you,
to protect you.'
and
'On their hands they will bear you up,
so that you will not dash your foot against a stone.'"

Satan backs up this temptation with a direct quote from Psalm 91:11, 12.

The **temptation**, once again, is to perform some feat that will prove Son-ship. The **issue** is the testing of God's integrity and faithfulness. Will God truly keep God's Word? The **truth** is, God is faithful and does not need to be put to the test.

Jesus draws once again upon God's Word as the source for his decision to not allow himself to be tempted. *"Again, it is written, 'Do not put the Lord your God to the test.'"* [Deuteronomy 6:16]

Jesus knew himself to be the Son of God, He had heard God announce his Son-ship at the Jordan River, He knew God's love for him through the outpouring of the Holy Spirit and, therefore, He did not need to put God's integrity and faithfulness to the test. The **temptation** is to put God to a test. The **issue** is trust. The **truth** is, God is faithful.

The Third Temptation: In the third temptation, Satan arrives at the real issue, which has to do with who is truly God and who is to be worshiped. Satan's desire from the beginning has been to usurp God's throne and be God himself. [Isaiah 14:12-15]

Therefore, Satan, the Adversary, is now more pointed in his tempting. The **temptation** is an appeal to the human desire for ownership, for power and for authority. The **issue**, however, is worship. The **truth** is that God alone is worthy of worship.

Satan took Jesus to the top of a high mountain and showed him the kingdoms of the world and their splendor.

"I will give you all their authority and splendor, for it has been given to me, and I can give it to anyone I want to. So, if you worship me, it will all be yours." [Luke 4:6, 7]

Jesus said to him,
"Away from me, Satan! For it is written, 'Worship the Lord your God, and serve him only.'" [Mathew 4:10; Deuteronomy 6:13]

Jesus later identified Satan as a liar and the father of lies. Lying is Satan's native language for there is no truth in him. [John 8:44] Thus, when Satan offered Jesus the kingdoms of the world, Jesus knew that they were not Satan's to offer.

At one point in his life as he prepared for his death on the cross, Jesus did refer to Satan as the 'ruler of this world,' [John 14:30]. However, being ruler and owner are two different things. Satan did not own the world and so it was not his to give away to anyone, especially to the Son of God, the Creator of the world.

Jesus knew who was worthy of worship, God alone. His words must have stung the adversary. *"Worship the Lord **your** God and serve him only."* Satan must also bow down to the God who created – and owns, the heavens and the earth. God alone is worthy of worship!

Victory: The Holy Spirit, working in the life of Jesus in the wilderness, brought victory. Satan, the Adversary, withdrew and angels came and ministered to Jesus there in the wilderness. Jesus had submitted himself to God. He remained in close fellowship with God through fasting and prayer. He allowed himself to be led by the Holy Spirit into the wilderness and to be tested by Satan. And it was in the wilderness that the Holy Spirit brought to his remembrance God's Word and promises. As a result, the Adversary, the tempter, withdrew from him *"until an opportune time."* [Luke 4:13]

That opportune time came when Satan later moved in the life of Judas who betrayed him, and in the life of Peter, causing him to deny Christ. The betrayal ultimately led to Jesus' death on the cross.

We Are Led and Tested by the Holy Spirit

If we are to be mature in every way and attain the fullness of the stature of Jesus Christ, then as we are baptized with the Holy Spirit, we must also allow the Spirit to lead us into and through the times of testing. At the same time, we must know, in truth, that we are Spirit led in all situations – especially those in which our faith is put to the test, the various wilderness experiences of our lives.

Godly wisdom will help us to understand that virtually every time we have a dynamic and powerful encounter with the Spirit of God, there will be a correlating encounter with the Adversary, Satan. Every time the Holy Spirit leads us in one direction, Satan will endeavor to lead us in another.

Every time we are filled with the Holy Spirit and know the joy and power of that filling, Satan will tempt us in ways that endeavor to rob us of both our joy and power.

One of the first things that happens after our spiritual birth is an inner struggle between our fleshly desires and our spiritual needs. Satan endeavors to put doubt into our minds. "**If** you really are a child of God you would not be thinking those kinds of thoughts anymore." "**If** you really are a new person you would not be acting like that." "**If** you really are converted and believe in Jesus, you wouldn't treat that person like that."

We must remember God's Word that declares that in Christ we are new creations. [II Corinthians 5:17] Therefore, *"everything old has passed away; see, everything has become new."* When the old ways – old habits, old thought patterns and old attitudes show up, they should serve only to remind us of the way we used to be, not the way we are now. As we mature in Christ, the Holy Spirit cleanses us of the old ways. That is God's amazing, sanctifying, cleansing grace.

Satan will also entice us to sin by saying, "If you really are forgiven for your sins, then you won't have to worry about that, so go ahead and do it." Or, to state it another way, "Did God really say that you should not do that?"

This is the type of question Satan asked of Eve regarding the fruit in the Garden of Eden. "Did God really say that?" which question causes us to wonder if we really have heard God correctly or maybe misunderstood that which we heard or, perhaps even misread and misunderstood the Word of God, the Scriptures. There are varieties of translations, you know!

In addition, the Adversary will endeavor to put doubt into our minds by questioning God's trustworthiness. "If God really is a good God and really cares for you, then why does God allow you to suffer?" "Why does God allow so much pain and evil in the world if God is a good God and the world belongs to God?" "If God really loves you, why are you always sick?"

Our thought life is Satan's battlefield. If a new convert listens to these words of the accuser, soon doubt will creep in and the new babe in Christ will begin to wonder if his/her conversion was for real and if God really does care. Even maturing Christians can be confronted with issues that may well create doubt and mistrust were it not for the presence and work of the Holy Spirit to strengthen and fortify them for the encounter.

Temptation and Accusation: Satan's two primary roles are to tempt and to accuse. His two greatest weapons are doubt and fear because both lead to unbelief and loss of faith.

It has been said that "fear motivates Satan in the same way that Faith motivates God." Any degree of fear will encourage Satan to continue harassment. As we express our faith in God – even our little faith, we discover the Holy Spirit leading us through the harassment to victory.

Jesus had a dynamic encounter with the Holy Spirit at the Jordan River when He was baptized. The Spirit immediately led him into the wilderness for a confrontation with Satan. He was involved in spiritual warfare.

Following that time when we experience being baptized with the Holy Spirit, there will be a time when we enter spiritual warfare with the Adversary. When we experience a release of God's power in our lives that sets the direction for our lives and ministry, there will be opposition from the one whose spiritual kingdom of darkness is being invaded by the Kingdom of Light.

Such opposition should not surprise us. The world is not in step with the Holy Spirit. Those who desire to be led by the Spirit and who try to keep in step with the Spirit, will experience opposition and even persecution from the world. In fact, that opposition may well come through persons who, it would seem, should know better.

That religious opposition became very real in the life of Sylvia who had a yearning to know more about the nature of God and a deep desire to experience the reality of God's Holy Spirit. She belonged to a strict and restrictive religious sect group that was opposed to its members receiving any information about the nature of God – and especially about the Holy Spirit, from any source other than the leaders or elders in the sect.

She registered for a seminar on the Holy Spirit that we were teaching in her area of the country. During the seminar, Sylvia came to me and stated that "when, not if, but when the members of her sect group found that she had attended the seminar she would be "dis-fellowshipped."

I was not familiar with the term at the time and so enquired what it meant. She said it meant that when they found out she had come to the seminar she would no longer be a part of the group nor would she have a family. She would be ostracized from the group and her family would disown her and consider her dead.

I asked her, "Then why did you come, knowing the consequences that awaited you?"

She responded, "Because I had to find out more about God. I knew there was more than what I was being taught. I wanted to know his Holy Spirit and experience his presence in my life."

She was being led by the Spirit even before she understood who is the Holy Spirit. The Holy Spirit created within her a hunger and thirsting for a deeper walk with God. Her hungering and thirsting for the things of God led her to step out on faith and seek that which would satisfy her spiritual hunger. Her faith was put to the test.

She later communicated that she had, indeed, been dis-fellowshipped from the religious group and consequently she had lost her family. However, she had gained a new and deeper relationship with God and the knowledge and experience of his Holy Spirit. Though she lost precious relationships with people she loved, she gained an eternal love relationship with Christ her Savior.

Such encounters and questioning of our faith commitment may well come from persons within the faith, or some sect within the faith, or even from some within our personal families. Our baptism with the Holy Spirit may well be questioned by persons within the community of faith who do not fully understand – or choose to not understand, God's Word at this point or to know how God's Holy Spirit works.

The opposition from within should come as no surprise. Jesus walked this path before us. His greatest opposition was not from those outside the community of faith, but from those within – even some within his personal family. Jesus' stoutest opposition came from those who were devoutly religious and staunch defenders of the traditional faith. In a word, Jesus was dis-fellowshipped by the very ones who should have understood, through his life, his works and his miracles, that He was who He said He was.

Spiritual Warfare: Spiritual warfare is not against flesh and blood. [Ephesians 6:12] Nor is it merely against the powers of darkness. It is also against the powers of entrenched religious traditions and mind-sets [strongholds] that would quench any new work of the Spirit of God. The newly baptized with the Holy Spirit child of God must be prepared for an encounter with both.

The study and knowing of God's Word, as well as fasting and prayer, are spiritual disciplines by which the Holy Spirit leads us into spiritual warfare. These disciplines enable us to draw nigh to God, know who we are in Christ, know that God does care for us and know what God has us do in the times of crisis as we draw on the power of His Holy Spirit.

God does not bring the difficult things upon us, any more than you or I would intentionally bring difficult things upon our children, but God's Word reminds us that we can:

""boast in our sufferings, knowing that suffering produces endurance, and endurance produces character, and character produces hope, and hope does not disappoint us, because God's love has been poured into our hearts through the Holy Spirit that has been given to us." [Romans 5:3-5]

We have the further assurance that:
"all things work together for good for those who love God, who are called according to his purpose." [Romans 8:28]

What Satan intends for harm, God works for good. The very things that Satan designs for our destruction are used by God to test and strengthen our faith. God will use these same experiences to purify our thoughts and motives, produce endurance and character, and renew our hope.

No difficult experience that comes into our lives goes to waste. God uses each one for our good.

To be filled with the Spirit of God does not mean that we will not be faced with temptations to sin. God's Word reminds us that temptation to sin is bound to come.

However, the Spirit of God can help us withstand the temptation.

"No testing has overtaken you that is not common to everyone. God is faithful, and he will not let you be tested beyond your strength, but with the testing he will also provide the way out so that you will be able to endure it." [I Corinthians 10:13]

In the hard times, the difficult situations, the tempting relationships the Holy Spirit leads those of us who will submit ourselves to God, and, in the process, make us stronger in our faith.

God cannot be tempted, and God does not tempt us, for that is not God's nature. We are tempted and enticed by our own evil desires.

"Then when that desire has conceived, it gives birth to sin and that sin, when it is fully grown, gives birth to death." [James 1:15]

The tempter often entices us through the weak areas of our lives – the desires of the flesh.

We must never be led to believe, however, that Satan cannot and will not attack us in those areas in which we pride ourselves in being strong. It is hazardous to our spiritual health to think or say, "Oh, I would never do anything like that," Or, "I have that issue settled and don't have to worry about it anymore."

Such attitudes often open the door for spiritual pride to set in which, in turn, makes real the possibility of a downfall.

When we are tempted to judge others for an area of weakness in their lives, we need to be careful lest we experience the same temptation. God's Word reminds us that

" if you think you are standing, watch out that you do not fall. No testing has overtaken you that is not common to everyone. God is faithful, and he will not let you be tested beyond your strength, but with the testing he will also provide the way out so that you may be able to endure it."
[I Corinthians 10:12, 13]

Jesus was tempted in every way, just as we are. Whatever fleshly temptation we face, Jesus faced it. Whatever sin dogs our lives, that very sin dogged Jesus also. The only difference between the path that Jesus walked here on earth and the one we walk is that Jesus did not sin.

The truth, however, is that the Holy Spirit provides a way and leads us through it, just as Jesus was led through it. It is important to understand that God never leads us **around** a temptation. God's Holy Spirit always leads us **through** the temptation so that when we have been led through it we will no longer be victims of the temptation but will be victors over it.

In those situations, the Holy Spirit comes as our Comforter. Com- [with] forte-[strength]. He comes to strengthen and fortify us to face whatever temptation with which we may be confronted and then gives us the power to overcome it.

When we are faced with temptation to sin, we must have the wisdom shown by Jesus and be able to differentiate between the **temptation** and the real **issue**. For example, we may be tempted to focus on self-fulfillment, self-gratification or self-preservation – "turning stones to bread," but the real issue may be one of doubting that God is able to provide for all our needs.

We may be tempted to do something just to prove that we are God's children and, as such, God will not allow us to be hurt or destroyed. For example, we will jump from "tall buildings," like choosing to give in to the temptation to get involved in immoral behavior, alternative lifestyles or to make unethical decisions, while trusting God to protect us from any negative consequences of such choices or decisions.

The real issue however, is not the **temptation** to jump from these "tall buildings." The **issue** is one of testing Gods integrity and faithfulness to God's own Word.

"Do not be deceived; God is not mocked, for you reap whatever you sow. If you sow to your own flesh, you will reap corruption from the flesh; but if you sow to the Spirit you will reap eternal life from the Spirit." [Galatians 6:7]

The **truth is**, we reap a harvest from the kinds of seeds we sow. Jesus quotes God's Word and it is a good Word to remember, *"Do not put God to the test."*

Likewise, the temptation may be one of pride, position, power, authority, recognition, status, wealth, name or self. The temptation may be the desire for one or all of these. However, the real issue is none of these. The real issue is worship.

To worship something is to acknowledge its absolute and true worth. That to which we acknowledge, and attribute absolute and true worth is that which we worship; and that which we worship is our god. That before which we spend most of our time is our idol. That into which we put most of our energy; that which occupies our thoughts, and which receives the greatest investment of our resources, is that which we worship. That which we worship is our god! Jesus makes it very clear that a person cannot serve God and money. [Matthew 6:24]

The **temptation** is one thing, the **issue** is another. During our wilderness experiences the Holy Spirit enables us to differentiate between the temptation and the issue and come to know the **truth** in the situation.

It is in those times that the Holy Spirit leads us to ask questions like, "What is at stake here?" "Am I questioning God's ability to provide?" "Am I calling into question God's integrity?" "Am I putting God to a foolish test?" "Am I seeking to worship God, or acknowledge my own self as the one of absolute and true worth and the only one on whom I can depend?" "Am I trying to be my own god?"

When we are led by the Holy Spirit into the wilderness areas of life, the Spirit teaches and instructs us in the ways of God when it comes to facing temptations and testing. As we trust the Spirit to lead us we find that we are better able to discern the issue behind the temptation and in that discernment say, as Jesus said, *"Away from me, Satan!"*

If we are to follow the example of Jesus, and by doing so grow up into Him, then we must allow ourselves to be led by the Holy Spirit. The Holy Spirit is the One who leads us to *"attain to the full measure of the stature of Christ."*

The Holy Spirit is the One who gives us new birth into the family of God and grows us up from spiritual infancy to maturity. The Holy Spirit is the One with whom we are baptized and given direction for our lives and ministry. The Holy Spirit is the One who leads us into all Truth for He is the Spirit of Truth.

As we are led by the Spirit we can face temptations that confront us. The Spirit then teaches us to submit ourselves to God, to rely upon God's Word for guidance. God gives us wisdom to discern the real issues behind the temptations, and to experience victory over the Adversary, Satan.

Life Application

Arnold found himself in relationship with a person who shared in the same kind of profession in which he was engaged and worked in the same office complex. Over a period of a few years they developed a very close friendship, sharing ideas regarding their profession, having lunch together, laughing, enjoying each other's company and generally depending on each other for mutual emotional support.

Though both were married, Arnold noticed that he had developed an emotional and physical attraction for this other person, who was sensitive, kind, understanding and always encouraging.

At first, he felt guilty that he was being unfaithful to his wife for having such an attraction to another person, but in time that feeling of guilt left as the other person exhibited the same kind of attraction to him.

Soon their mutual feelings surfaced, and they realized that they were "drawn" to each other and began to share their feelings with each other.

They ultimately concluded that their feelings for each other were real and that they "were meant for each other." Even though they were both in a committed relationship with their respective spouses they felt like they were "soul mates" and their relationship had a spiritual quality about it.

The Spirit of God – though Arnold did not realize at the time that it was the Spirit, put it into his heart to seek counsel. He thought that perhaps he should talk with someone about his feelings to get an objective insight into the relationship he had developed with his co-worker

After hearing Arnold's story, I, as the counselor, simply encouraged him to first seek the guidance of God's Word and God's Holy Spirit to discover what, according to God's Word, is the right and righteous thing for him to do. Arnold, being a man with a workable knowledge of Jesus and a certain level of faith in God, began to explore his feelings and his attraction for his co-worker, while at the same time becoming more familiar with God's Word that is related to such relationships as the one in which he found himself.

He could not deny his feelings. To him they were real, and they were valid. However, in time and with more counseling with me and with others, the Holy Spirit led Arnold to decide – a difficult decision, but, for him, a necessary one.

That decision was to ask the Holy Spirit to help him differentiate between feelings based on emotional needs and personal gratification, and feelings based on commitment and love that has to do with what is right and true from God's perspective.

Ultimately, the Holy Spirit helped Arnold to make that differentiation. He could look upon his co-worker as a person of true value and worth; one for whom he had deep feelings of admiration and concern, but now as a sister in Christ and not as someone to fill an emotional need or void in his own life.

He was later able to share with his co-worker the admiration and respect that he had for her, but at the same time the necessity to make the decision to break off the relationship that he knew to be wrong.

Having once made that decision, the Holy Spirit helped Arnold to experience a deeper walk with God, a keener trust in God's Word and an even greater commitment to his wife of many years.

This did not happen overnight, nor even in a brief span of weeks or months. The battle between the temptation, the issue and the truth still surface on occasion, but now Arnold knows where to turn for guidance. He, as did Jesus, turns to the Word of God, and finds, as with Jesus, that Satan leaves him *"until an opportune time."* [Luke 4:13]

For Satan and Jesus, that "opportune time" came when Satan caused two of Jesus' friends to deny him [Peter] and turn against him [Judas]. Perhaps this is one reason why Jesus, on a few occasions, cautions his disciples to "watch," or "be alert."

The apostle Peter writes,

"Discipline yourselves, keep alert. Like a roaring lion your adversary the devil prowls around, looking for someone to devour. Resist him, steadfast in your faith for you know that your brothers and sisters in all the world are undergoing the same kinds of suffering." [I Peter 5:8, 9]

PERSONAL REFLECTION

Take time for personal reflection upon the following Scriptures:

"Jesus was led by the Spirit in the wilderness." [Luke 4:1 NIV]

"If we live by the Spirit, let us also be guided by the Spirit." [Galatians 5:25]

TAKE TIME TO REFLECT UPON THIS THOUGHT

"When the old ways show up, they remind me of the way I used to be, not the way I am now." What are some of the "old ways" that show up on occasion and how do I handle them?

_____
_____
_____

A TIME TO REMEMBER

1. The time when I was faced with the difficult decision to resist temptation to:

   _____

2. This is how I remember the Holy Spirit leading me in that time.

   _____

3. The temptation was: _____
4. The issue was: _____
5. Some of my wilderness experiences are:

   _____
   _____

6. This is how God's Word helped me in some of the hard times:
   _____
   _____

7. This is what "being led and tested by the Spirit" means to me:
   _____
   _____
   _____

8. These have been my experiences with fasting and prayer:
   _____
   _____

9. These difficult experiences in my life have resulted in a stronger faith and commitment to God:
   _____
   _____

10. These Scriptures have proven to be a source of strength to me in times of temptation, doubt, fear, and questioning.
    _____
    _____
    _____

Prayer: "O God, I acknowledge your absolute and true worth. You alone are worthy of worship. You alone are God.

Forgive me when I fail to trust you completely and fall prey to the temptation to rely on myself and my own feelings. Forgive my sin of rebellion and disobedience. Teach me to be like your Son, Jesus. Fill me with your Holy Spirit that I may stand strong in the hard times and times of temptation. Teach me to hold to my faith in You. Amen."

CHAPTER 5

EMPOWERED BY THE SPIRIT

"Then Jesus, filled with the power of the Spirit, returned to Galilee, and a report about him spread through all the surrounding country. He began to teach in their synagogues and was praised by everyone." [Luke 4:14, 15]

"Jesus went throughout Galilee, teaching in their synagogues, and proclaiming the good news of the kingdom and curing every disease and every sickness among the people. So, his fame spread throughout all Syria, and they brought to him all the sick, those who were afflicted with various diseases and pains, demoniacs, epileptics, and paralytics, and he cured them." [Matthew 4:23, 24]

Jesus spent forty days and nights in the wilderness fasting, praying and being tempted by his Adversary, the devil. We are told in Scripture that when the devil had finished all his tempting, angels came and waited on Jesus. [Matthew 4:11]

Jesus had resisted the temptation to take matters into his own hands. He put his trust in God to care for his needs and, as a result, his needs were met. He resisted the temptation to exalt himself and, as a result, he was exalted by God. He resisted the temptation to put God to the test and, as a result, God's faithfulness, without being tested, was proven by God himself.

When Jesus came out of the wilderness, he returned to Galilee *"in the power of the Holy Spirit."* [Luke 4:14, 15 NIV]

During the three years of his public earthly ministry all the spiritual gifts of the Holy Spirit, that are listed in I Corinthians 12:7-11, functioned in power in Jesus' life.

Wisdom. Jesus manifested the gift of wisdom. He was known throughout his ministry for his wisdom that far exceeded that of his contemporaries. At the age of twelve he was in the Temple courts in Jerusalem sitting among the elders and discussing with them the things of God. Everyone was amazed at his understanding and his answers. [Luke 2:46, 47] Already his wisdom was being sharpened by the Spirit of God.

On one of his trips to his hometown during his adult life, *"he began teaching the people in their synagogue, and they were amazed. 'Where did this man get this wisdom and these deeds of power."* [Matthew 13:54; Mark 6:1-6]

His wisdom was acknowledged by his neighbors. However, they took offense at him because they knew him to be simply a home-town boy who had grown up in their midst. They could not understand where he had gotten his wisdom and so, had difficulty accepting it.

The gift of wisdom was demonstrated on many occasions as Jesus was confronted by those who endeavored to trap him in his words. He used wisdom when he dealt with the question of whether it was right to pay taxes to Caesar. [Matthew 22:15-22]

Wisdom was demonstrated as he showed the Sadducees, who did not believe in the resurrection that, according to Scripture and the nature of God, there is a resurrection from the dead. [Matthew 22:23-33] He demonstrated wisdom in his teachings and in the questions he asked, as he called on the Pharisees to think about whose son is the Christ. [Matthew 22:41-46] They could not answer his question and from then on did not choose to ask him any more questions because they could not withstand his wisdom.

That same level of wisdom is available to believers as they endeavor to live out their lives in relationship with their God, their family, their co-workers and others with whom they may relate.

Teresa is a gifted child of God who demonstrates wisdom beyond her years. Whenever there are discussions surrounding decisions that need to be made in her family, or ministry to someone in need, or need for clarification in business meetings, she is always able to shed light and clear understanding of the situation at hand. God has given her the supernatural gift of wisdom simply because she seeks his counsel and direction.

Knowledge. Jesus was also empowered with the word of knowledge. On several occasions he manifested this gift that revealed to him things that were hidden from others; things that enabled him to fulfill the ministry to which God had called him. The Holy Spirit empowered Jesus with the gift of knowledge. This spiritual gift functioned in Jesus' life and throughout his ministry.

When he talked with the Samaritan woman at the well, he revealed to her that she had had five husbands and the one with whom she was now living was not her husband. [John 4] As a result of that revelation, she witnessed to her village of Sychar. The villagers came out to hear him, he stayed with them two days and many of the villagers became believers.

Jesus told Nathaniel that he had seen him while he was sitting under a fig tree. Presumably, he saw him, not as you and I would see someone, but rather by supernatural knowledge, because it elicited from Nathaniel the declaration that Jesus was truly the Son of God and King of Israel. [John 1:44-51]

When he came upon a home where a little girl had died, He reminded the crowd of mourners that she was not dead but only sleeping They were offended by his remarks and laughed at him for they knew her to be dead. Yet Jesus went to her and raised her up from her bed and back to life.

Jesus had knowledge of something that was not known to the others. As a result, he restored life to the little girl. [Matthew 9:18-26]

Jesus, the focus of whose life was continually upon God, knew what was in the heart of God. He could even say at one point,

"Very truly I tell you, the Son can do nothing on his own, but only what he sees the Father doing; for whatever the Father does, the Son does likewise." [John 5:19]

On another occasion he said, *"What I speak therefore, I speak just as the Father has told me.""* [John 12:50b]

The gift of knowledge is an essential and primary gift if a person is to be in ministry in the Name of Jesus. My wife, Audrey, was blessed with the ability to seek and receive direction from God on how to pray for people. Whenever we were in ministry to someone in need, we recognized the fact that we, on our own, did not know how to give adequate counsel or how to pray. We learned the truth of Romans 8:26,

"The Spirit helps us in our weakness; for we do not know how to pray as we ought, but that very Spirit intercedes with sighs too deep for words."

Therefore, before praying, we ask "God, what do you want us to say to this person" or "how do you want us to pray for this person?" Then we listen. She was receptive in listening to and hearing God speak to her spirit, giving the direction requested. He imparts the knowledge needed to make the ministry more effective.

Faith: Jesus lived by faith. He preached faith. He demonstrated faith. He was faith personified. He was continually revealing the meaning of living by faith. *"Now faith is the assurance of things hoped for, the conviction of things not seen."* [Hebrews 11:1]

Jesus endeavored to instruct his followers to live by the conviction that "believing is seeing," and not as the world lived, by seeing, then believing.

Jesus continually reminded his disciples to exercise their faith, to have faith in God, to have faith the size of a mustard seed and see mountains be moved. He affirmed persons who demonstrated the slightest degree of faith and rebuked those who did not walk by faith.

The Holy Spirit empowered Jesus with the gift of faith that enabled him to have absolute confidence and trust in God, know that he could be assured of the things for which God had planned and confident of things that Jesus could not yet see. He was empowered by and lived by faith!

Healing: Jesus was also empowered with the gifts of healing. It is estimated that ninety-five percent of Jesus' ministry involved healing of some kind. He had a concern for the whole person – spirit, soul, body and relationships. [John 7:23] He also set about to free those who experienced bondage to the demonic. He drove out unclean and evil spirits.

One hundred percent of his ministry involved deliverance, because he was continually delivering people out of darkness into light, out of ignorance into understanding, out of the Lie into the Truth, out from being lost to being found, out of sickness into health, out of brokenness into wholeness, out of the kingdom of this world into the Kingdom of God.

About twenty five percent of his ministry involved deliverance of people from bondage to demonic and unclean spirits. He truly came as Deliverer.

"Jesus went throughout Galilee, teaching in their synagogues, and proclaiming the good news of the kingdom and curing every disease and every sickness among the people. So, his fame spread throughout all Syria, and they brought to him all the sick, those who were afflicted with various diseases and pains, demoniacs, epileptics, and paralytics, and he cured them. And great crowds followed him from Galilee, the Decapolis, Jerusalem, Judea, and from beyond the Jordan." [Matthew 4:23-25]

Wherever he went people responded to his presence by bringing themselves or family members or neighbors to him for healing. *"One day as he was teaching...the power of the Lord was with him to heal"* He then healed a paralytic. [Luke 5:17ff]

Jesus did not heal everyone who was ill. However, Jesus did heal everyone who was ill and who came to him for healing. He even healed some who did not come to him themselves, but whose healing was requested by members of their families – as with the centurion's servant who lay ill at home and the centurion came to Jesus to ask for him to come and heal his servant. [Luke 7:1-11] Jesus simply told the centurion to go home because his servant is healed.

A similar thing happened with the synagogue ruler's daughter [Mark 5:21ff] as Jesus went to her and spoke healing, raising her from the dead in this case, upon the request of the father.

He also healed at least one person who did not seek healing from him. A man with a shriveled hand was in the synagogue where Jesus was debating with the religious leaders as to whether it was lawful to heal on the Sabbath. Jesus told the man to stretch out his hand. He obediently did so, and his hand was completely restored. [Luke 6:6-10]

We have only to read the Gospel accounts of Jesus' life and ministry to see where the spiritual gift of healings was functioning from the time of his coming out of the wilderness to the time when He died on the cross. Even there He ministered spiritual healing to the very crowd who crucified him as he interceded on their behalf for their forgiveness. He also brought spiritual healing to the thief who hung beside him on another cross by reassuring him that he would share with him in paradise.

Lisa was a six-year-old girl who was diagnosed by the medical profession with a tumor on one of her kidneys. Surgery was scheduled to remove the kidney. The parents asked if I, as their pastor, would travel with them to Children's Hospital in Seattle, WA, and be with them during the surgery.

While on the ferry that traveled across Puget Sound to Seattle, we prayed, asking God to remove the tumor and restore total health to Lisa. Arriving at the hospital, her parents took her to be prepared for surgery and I remained in the waiting area.

Much to my surprise, within a very short time, perhaps an hour, all three of them returned to the waiting room. I inquired as to what had happened? They shared that after thorough examination and further tests it was discovered that the tumor was no longer on her kidney. The original X-rays and current X-rays revealed two different things. The tumor had just "disappeared."

Lisa is now a grown woman, loving wife and mother and a very productive, professional artist, who blesses the lives of many through the gifts and faith that God has given to her

Miracles: The Holy Spirit empowered Jesus to work miracles. The ministry of Jesus was marked by Holy Spirit power. From the time He came out of the wilderness He demonstrated supernatural power as He worked miracles of healing the sick, making the lame walk, the blind to see the deaf hear and the maimed restored. [Matthew 4:23-25]

He also calmed storms on the Sea of Galilee [Mark 4:35-41], turned water into wine at a wedding in Cana, [John 2:1-11] and raised people from the dead. [John 11:38-44]

Many people believed in Jesus because of the miraculous signs that he did. [John 2:23] Others saw the miracles as proof that Jesus had come from God. [John 3:2] Still others saw the miraculous things that Jesus did as a sign that he was the Prophet that God had promised to Moses. [Deuteronomy 18:18, John 6:14] Many felt that he was the Christ of God because of the miracles. [John 7:31]

Many crowds of people followed Jesus *"because they saw the miraculous signs he had performed on the sick."* [John 6:2 NIV]

At one point, Jesus chastised the crowd by telling them, *"Unless you people see miraculous signs and wonders you will never believe."* [John 4:48 NIV]

Regardless of the miraculous signs and wonders that Jesus performed during his ministry, there were many who simply would not believe in him. *"Although he had performed so many signs in their presence, they did not believe in him."* [John 12:37] Two verses later, it is recorded that they "*could not believe.*" [John 12:39] Unbelief soon led to inability to believe.

A miracle - even that of raising someone from the dead, did not move them to belief. Jesus had already known this and stated that *"If they do not listen to Moses and the prophets, neither will they be convinced if someone rises from the dead.'"* [Luke 16:31]

Jesus had a miracle-filled ministry and his miraculous powers were demonstrated as he took control of situations in human life as well as the elements of nature around him.

Prophecy: Jesus was also empowered with the gift of prophecy and was acknowledged by many as a prophet. The office of prophet had not been exercised in the Jewish community of faith for approximately four hundred years. Now, in one generation, two prophets arrive on the scene:

John the Baptist and Jesus. Both men are acknowledged by the people as prophets.

The power to work miracles is one evidence of a person having prophetic credentials. It was because Jesus worked many miracles in the presence of the people that he was acclaimed by some as a prophet and by others as The Prophet foretold in the time of Moses [Deuteronomy 18:18].

Jesus evidently saw himself in the prophet's role. On one occasion when he was being questioned and opposed by people in his home town, he said, *"Prophets are not without honor except in their own country and in their own house."* [Matthew 13:57]

The prophetic gift functioned in Jesus' life as he spoke to the people of the Kingdom of God. He spoke the inspired Word of God. in true prophetic fashion he encouraged the people, strengthened them, comforted them and instructed them in the ways of God.

Also, in true prophetic fashion, he corrected and rebuked those who needed it without regard to status or position.

The prophets who preceded Jesus – Elijah, Elisha, Isaiah, Jeremiah, Daniel, Ezekiel, Joel, and all the others including John the Baptist, experienced the power of the Holy Spirit in their lives as they spoke the inspired messages that God had given them to speak. When God's Spirit came upon them, they were in direct communication with God and felt called to warn the nation of Israel of the consequences of sin, give guidance regarding moral issues and to call the community back into right relationship with God.

In the years prior to the coming of Jesus, priests and kings, as well as prophets, were also anointed and empowered by the Holy Spirit to fulfill the offices in which they served.

Like the prophets of old, Jesus fulfilled the prophetic office by reminding the people of the consequences of their sin. He called them back into right relationship with God.

Jesus exercised this prophetic role as he, late in his ministry, looked over the holy city of Jerusalem:

"As he came near and saw the city, he wept over it, saying, "If you, even you, had only recognized on this day the things that make for peace! But now they are hidden from your eyes. Indeed, the days will come upon you, when your enemies will set up ramparts around you and surround you and hem you in on every side. They will crush you to the ground, you and your children within you, and they will not leave within you one stone upon

another; because you did not recognize the time of your visitation from God." [Luke 19:41-44]

This prophetic word was fulfilled about 40 years later, for in 70 A.D. Rome sacked and destroyed the holy city and the temple.

He felt responsibility to teach them and give them guidance relative to making right ethical and moral decisions. His messages and his actions were Spirit-inspired and Spirit-motivated.

Like the priests and kings of old, Jesus was acknowledged by the early church as Priest and King.

He is seen as a priest after the order of Melchizedek, whose priesthood is *"through the power of an indestructible life."* [Hebrews 7:16] And *"because Jesus lives forever, he has a permanent priesthood. Therefore, he is able to save completely those who come to God through him, because he always lives to intercede for them."* [Hebrews 7:24, 25 NIV]

The early church also saw Jesus as King of kings and Lord of lords. [Revelation 17:14, 19:16;] Jesus saw himself as King. In his conversation with Pilate prior to his crucifixion, Pilate asked, *"Are you the king of the Jews? He answered, "You say so."* [Luke 23:3]

He fulfilled the offices of Prophet, Priest and King – anointed by God and empowered by the Holy Spirit.

When Jesus came out of the wilderness, he returned to Galilee in the power of the Holy Spirit, empowered to preach the Kingdom of God and to make it a reality in his own time. His Spirit-empowered message was the same as that of John the Baptist: *"Repent, for the kingdom of heaven has come near,"* or *"at hand,"* as some versions of Scripture state. [Matthew 3:2; 4:17]

Prophets of old told of the Kingdom of God that is "to come." John the Baptist preached that the Kingdom of God is "at hand." Jesus preached that the Kingdom of Heaven is *"within* [or among] *you."* It is here!

Discernment: As Jesus walked in the power of the Holy Spirit, he also exercised the spiritual gift of discernment, or the ability to distinguish between spirits. Throughout his ministry he encountered persons who were in bondage to the demonic. They were imprisoned in fear, experienced physical seizures, manifested superhuman destructive powers and were generally harassed by the evil one, Satan.

Jesus discerned their need for freedom, came against the force that held them hostage and delivered them. As a result, he healed the demoniac, [Luke 8:26-39] as well as a boy with an evil spirit that threw him into convulsions and seizures. [Luke 9:37-45] He set free a crippled woman who had been in bondage to Satan for many years. [Luke 13:10-13]

Jesus healed a blind and mute man who was demon-possessed [Matthew 12:22]. At another time he healed a deaf and mute man who was not demon-possessed but had a physical malady [Mrk7:31-37] In each case He was able to discern the source of the sickness and the appropriate action to take in facilitating the healing.

Jesus was also able to discern what was in the hearts of people. He discerned who would betray him before it happened. [Luke 22:21, 22] He knew who would deny him before he was denied. [John 13:38] He knew that he would be crucified before he was crucified. [Mark 10:32-34] He knew that he would be raised from the dead before he was dead. [Mark 10:34] He discerned the thoughts of those around him. [Mark 2:8]

The Gospel writer John reports that while Jesus was in Jerusalem at the Passover Feast,

"many believed in his name because they saw the signs that he was doing. But Jesus on his part would not entrust himself to them, because he knew all people and needed no one to testify about anyone; for he himself knew what was in everyone." [John 2:23-25]

Discernment is the ability to tell if something within a person is from God or Satan or has a human origin. The gift of discernment enabled Jesus to identify the source and thus provide the cure or give the appropriate response to the situation at hand.

Tongues: There is no clear evidence in Scripture that Jesus manifested the spiritual gift of speaking in tongues or interpreting tongues. However, it may be presumed that he did, for in the Gospel of Mark it is reported that Jesus said, *"by using my name they will cast out demons, they will speak in new tongues."* [Mark 16:17]

Jesus never asked his disciples to do anything that he had not done or was unwilling to do. Therefore, it may be assumed that Jesus spoke in tongues even as he spoke three known languages: Hebrew, perhaps Latin and Aramaic. He spoke the language of people and that of angels.

Interpretation of Tongues: At Pentecost, following the outpouring of the Holy Spirit upon the disciples, they went out into the streets of Jerusalem proclaiming the good news of the Kingdom of God. [Acts 2:1-13] There were at least fifteen people groups gathered in Jerusalem for the feast of Unleavened Bread, concluding with Pentecost - the fiftieth day after the celebration of Passover.

Each of the people groups heard the apostles speaking in their own language, even though the apostles were all from Galilee. As they spoke the good news, the people who had gathered from other countries could understand it.

The Holy Spirit interpreted the message, spoken in what was probably Hebrew or Aramaic, into the familiar language of the people.

A similar thing happened to me. While speaking to a group of youth at a conference about speaking in tongues, I asked how many had had the experience. Out of the approximately one hundred in attendance, about ten or fifteen had experienced speaking in tongues or had heard someone pray in tongues. I told the youth that I wanted to lead them in prayer, closing by praying "in the Spirit" or praying "in tongues," so that they would have the experience of hearing tongues.

There was one girl student in the group who had been raised in the Jewish faith. She attended the conference because she desired to know Jesus as her Messiah. She had little or no understanding of the Holy Spirit or spiritual gifts.

She came to me after the workshop and asked me why I had chosen to speak in Hebrew and tell the youth that I had spoken in tongues? I asked her what caused her to think that I had done that. She replied that in the prayer I prayed I had recited a Hebrew prayer that she had learned when a child and as I recited it I had made some mistakes in part of the prayer. The mistakes had caught her attention. She felt that if I was going to say the prayer, I should practice getting it right and to tell the youth that I would be praying in Hebrew.

I asked her if she believed in the Holy Spirit and the supernatural gift of speaking in tongues and she told me "No, this was all new to her."

I then informed her that I had never learned the Hebrew language and I do not speak Hebrew. Therefore, what she heard was what God wanted her to hear, including the mistakes. Perhaps it was for getting her attention and letting her know that he is able, in whatever way it takes, to reach into a person's life, to bring new understanding of his power and ability to transform our lives.

Her understanding of God's ability to enable us to speak in languages we do not know, to help others come to Christ, was increased greatly and she came to a new appreciation of the power of God's Holy Spirit.

Tongues and the interpretation of tongues worked a miracle on Pentecost and three thousand people came to receive Jesus as their Messiah, their Lord and their Savior.

Jesus came out of the wilderness experience and returned to Galilee in the power of the Holy Spirit. From that point on, until his Ascension, He was engaged in a Spirit-empowered ministry that moved him to preach the Kingdom of God, teach about Kingdom living, heal the sick and deliver the demon-possessed.

Jesus gave that same ministry to his disciples. When he sent the Twelve Disciples out into ministry,

"Then Jesus called the twelve together and gave them power and authority over all demons and to cure diseases, and he sent them out to proclaim the kingdom of God and to heal." [Luke 9:1, 2]

Later He sent out seventy-two others with the same instructions: *"cure the sick who are there, and say to them, "The kingdom of God has come near to you."* [Luke 10:9]

As the disciples went out in ministry they experienced the power of the Spirit moving in and through them. They returned to Jesus rejoicing and saying, *"Lord, in your name even the demons submit to us!"* [Luke 10:17]

Following the day of Pentecost, after the Holy Spirit had come upon the disciples in the Upper Room, they experienced the supernatural power that Jesus had promised them. They went forth that day in the power of the Spirit proclaiming the good news of the Kingdom of God and healing the sick. The supernatural gifts of the Holy Spirit were manifested in their lives as they were in the life of Jesus. As a result, *"And day by day the Lord added to their number those who were being saved."* [Acts 2:47]

Ministering in the Power of the Holy Spirit

If we, as disciples of Jesus Christ, are to *"attain to the measure of the full stature of Christ"* and *"grow up into Him who is our Head,"* then we must walk in the power of the Holy Spirit as did He.

The work of ministry cannot be accomplished through human effort alone. God has designed that the work of the church – the preaching of the Kingdom of God, the teaching of Kingdom living, the healing of the sick and delivering persons from bondage to the demonic, can only be accomplished through the empowering work of God's Holy Spirit.

The supernatural work of the Kingdom of God requires that the supernatural gifts of God's Holy Spirit be used to make the supernatural Kingdom manifest in our midst and visible to the natural world around us.

We are to be open to allowing all the gifts of the Holy Spirit to work in and through our lives. We cannot be selective about which gift we do or do not want, for in attempting to do so we quench the Spirit and we lose the power.

As the Holy Spirit manifests the gifts of knowledge, wisdom and discernment through us we find ourselves to be attuned to the heart and mind of God. Only the Holy Spirit knows the thoughts of God. [I Corinthians 2:11]

The only way we can know the thoughts of God is to allow the Holy Spirit of God to reveal them to us through these supernatural gifts. Only by using the gift of spiritual discernment can we distinguish that which is of God and that which is not of God.

As we allow the spiritual gifts of prophecy and tongues to be manifest in our lives we can experience the supernatural power of the Holy Spirit speaking through us to bring that word of God that changes human lives and circumstances.

Pleasant sounding messages and politically correct statements do not work the miracle of change in human existence. God's inspired word, however, convicts and changes human hearts, which in turn changes the nature of human behavior and existence.

We can praise God in our native tongues and our hearts rejoice. Nevertheless, when we submit our tongues to the move of the Spirit of God and allow the Spirit to praise God through us, it brings rejoicing to the heart of God.

The Holy Spirit is the only One who can enable us to worship in spirit and in truth. God seeks such to worship. [John 4:23, 24]

The spiritual gifts of faith, miracles and healing are gifts of the Holy Spirit that empower us to be engaged in the overt ministry of bringing healing and wholeness to persons' lives. These are all outward manifestations of the Gospel that is preached. They are the powerful gifts that enable justice to happen. They are the gifts that turn potentially destructive conditions into positive and productive happenings.

Without the supernatural empowerment of the Holy Spirit there are no supernatural miracles and there are no supernatural healings, regardless of the amount of faith that may be demonstrated. Even faith itself is a gift of the Spirit.

If the Church, individually and collectively, is to experience the *"to the measure of the full stature of Jesus Christ,"* then it must allow the Holy Spirit to work in its life and ministry in the same way in which the Spirit worked in the life and ministry of Jesus – wholeheartedly and without reservation.

That which Jesus promised to the disciples, He had already experienced when he walked out of the wilderness – the power of the Holy Spirit.

Thus, He spoke to the disciples, *"You will receive power when the Holy Spirit has come upon you...."* [Acts 1:8]

That which he manifested in his life and ministry and that which he promised to the disciples, is still available to all who will receive: *"You will receive power when the Holy Spirit has come upon you."*

Holy Spirit power is the supernatural power of God who enables us, as the body of Christ, to do the supernatural ministry of the supernatural church to preach the supernatural Gospel of Jesus Christ, heal the sick, forgive sins and drive out demons from the lives of those who live in the natural world.

Life Application

Larry, a district judge, and his wife were scheduled to host a delegation of visiting foreign dignitaries. It was to be a very formal dinner affair. At the time of the dinner he remembered that he had also committed himself to be present at his church for a spiritual renewal weekend. He had double-booked his calendar.

At the time for the dinner, he felt compelled to excuse himself, apologize to his wife, leave her to host the dinner and for him to attend the opening session of the spiritual renewal event at his church. For some unexplainable reason, he knew he must be there.

During the service I made the statement that it is important to allow God's Holy Spirit to be released in our lives so that we may experience supernatural power to fulfill the work that God has called us to do in whatever venue of work we may find ourselves. Otherwise, we are working under our own abilities and not with the power of God.

After the evening session was concluded, he came to me and said that he had never known the release of that power in his life and desired that it should happen. As we prayed together, the judge experienced baptism with the Holy Spirit, the welling up of great joy within his life and a "release of the Spirit" that he had not known before. He also experienced a release of uncontainable joy welling up from within his innermost being.

When he went home and explained to his wife, who was also a committed Believer, why he had to do what he did and what happened as a result, to his amazement, she understood. She had been praying for that to happen so that her husband could know the joy of walking in the Spirit. God had graciously provided an answer to her prayers. The dinner event had been a success with his wife hosting it and the judge experienced a new walk with his Lord. Both he and his wife were richly blessed.

A year later I was back at that same church for another spiritual renewal weekend. During one of the sharing sessions the judge gave witness to what power had been released in his life in the past year. Since he had experienced being baptized with the Holy Spirit the previous year, he had been overwhelmed with the wisdom that had suddenly become evident as he made important decisions in his courtroom.

He had new and clearer insights into the law and found it much easier to interpret the law and make it applicable to cases.

The supernatural gifts of wisdom and knowledge had empowered him to become a better district judge. He felt as though he were able to draw on supernatural resources for help in the work that God had given him to do in the practical, everyday issues with which he was faced.

He knew he was assisted by the One who is the Judge of all things to understand the few things about which he was called to make judgments.

He came out of his own personal, spiritual wilderness empowered by the Holy Spirit to be about his work. He knew the reality of Jesus' teaching: *"You will receive power when the Holy Spirit has come upon you."* [Acts 1:8]

PERSONAL REFLECTION

Take time to reflect and meditate on the following Scriptures. Think about how you are to fulfill the commission that Jesus has given you.

"Jesus called the twelve together and gave them power and authority over all demons and to cure diseases, and he sent them out to proclaim the kingdom of God and to heal." [Luke 9:1,2]

"After this the Lord appointed seventy others and sent them on ahead of him in pairs to every town and place where he himself intended to go......Whenever you enter a town and its people welcome you, eat what is

set before you; cure the sick who are there, and say to them, "The Kingdom of God has come near to you." [Luke 10:1, 8, 9]

"All authority in heaven and on earth has been given to me. Go therefore and make disciples of all nations, baptizing them in the name of the Father and of the Son and of the Holy Spirit, and teaching them to obey everything I have commanded you. And remember, I am with you always, to the end of the age." [Matthew 28:18-20]

Think about: "Will I be able to do this? How am I to preach the Kingdom of God and heal the sick? How do I go about making disciples for Jesus? How am I to drive out demons?" Can I do it in my own power and with my own talents?

When Jesus said, *"I am with you always,"* does that mean that I am in co-ministry with him? If so, how do I allow that to happen in my life?

It happens as we allow the power of the Holy Spirit to be released in our lives, as was present in Jesus' life, to accomplish the work he has for us to do.

A TIME TO REMEMBER

1. After a wilderness experience in my life, I experienced new power from the Holy Spirit in these ways: _____
2. I have experienced the following Spiritual Gifts manifested I\in my life:
    a. Wisdom
    b. Knowledge
    c. Faith
    d. Gifts of healing
    e. Miraculous powers
    f. Prophecy
    g. Discernment
    h. Tongues
    I. Interpretation of Tongues
3. If you have not experienced any one of the empowering gifts of the Holy Spirit that are listed above, write how you feel about that and express your willingness [or hesitancy] in allowing that gift, or gifts, to be manifested in your life.

PRAYER

"O God, you are the Source of all Life and all Power. You have given me your Son, Jesus as my Savior and Friend. You have poured out your Holy Spirit upon my life and I am now able to call you "Abba." I know that I am your child and co-heir with Jesus of your Kingdom.

"You have called me, as a disciple of Jesus, to preach your Kingdom, heal the sick and deliver people from bondage to the evil one. You know that on my own I am powerless to do that which you have asked me to do.

"I ask you to release the power of your Holy Spirit in my life. Release the spiritual gifts in me so that I may experience all that is necessary to fulfill the work you have called me to do. I may not fully understand the purpose of the gifts, but I know that you have designed them so that I may be empowered to proclaim your good news and heal the sick.

"Thank you for releasing your Holy Spirit's power in my life. I thank you in the Name of Jesus. Amen"

CHAPTER 6

ANOINTED BY THE SPIRIT

"When he [Jesus], came to Nazareth, where he had been brought up, he went to the synagogue on the Sabbath day, as was his custom. He stood up to read, and the scroll of the prophet Isaiah was given to him. He unrolled the scroll and found the place where it was written:
The Spirit of the Lord is upon me because He has anointed me.
to bring good news to the poor.
He has sent me to proclaim release to the captives,
and recovery of sight to the blind,
to let the oppressed, go free,
to proclaim the year of the Lord's favor."
[Luke 4:16-19]

Jesus was conceived and born of the Holy Spirit. He grew up in the Spirit. He was baptized with the Spirit. He was led into and through the wilderness by the Spirit. He came out of the wilderness in the power of the Holy Spirit. Jesus was also anointed by the Holy Spirit.

The practice of anointing with oil reaches back into antiquity in both secular and religious traditions. Persons have anointed their skin with oil to keep it soft in dry climates. Oil has been used for cooking, as perfumes, as medicine, as a cosmetic and to prepare bodies for burial.

The anointing with oil – especially olive oil, and specifically in the traditions of Jews and Christians, has been used for sacred purposes and is usually associated with the consecration of individuals or items for specific religious duties or purposes.

To be anointed is to be consecrated. To be consecrated is to be set apart for sacred purposes and uses. Certain vessels, buildings and places were anointed with oil and set apart for common to sacred uses.

Anointed Individuals: Among the ancient Hebrew people, prophets, priests and kings were anointed, consecrated and set apart for their various responsibilities to God and to the community of faith. They were ordained to function in a capacity apart from the common work of others. They were representatives and spokespersons for God. The prophets spoke to the people on behalf of God. The priests spoke to God on behalf of the people. The kings ruled over the people, providing safety and security, as representatives of God, making sure that the people followed God's laws.

As consecrated leaders, they were authorized to carry out the work of their various offices. The anointing carried with it the authority to fulfill the role for which they had been set apart. When Samuel anointed Saul as King of Israel, Saul was given authority to govern as king and theocratic vassal of the Lord. [I Samuel 9:16; 16:3]

During the earlier years, kings were anointed by prophets. This responsibility apparently later became the privilege of the priests. [I Kings 1:39; II Kings 11:12]

Jesus' Anointing: When Jesus began his public ministry, He went to the synagogue in Nazareth, his home town. He stood to read as the Scroll of the Prophet Isaiah was handed to him. He unrolled the scroll to what is now Isaiah 61 and read: *"The Spirit of the Lord is upon me, because He has anointed me......* [Isaiah 61:1, 2; Luke 4:18, 19]

Jesus was anointed, not by human prophets or priests, but by the Holy Spirit of God. He was anointed – authorized by the Spirit of God, to bring good news to the poor, heal the sick and free all those who were under the power of the devil.

The message of Peter in the home of Cornelius summarizes Jesus' powerful and authoritative ministry:

"You know the message he sent to the people of Israel, preaching peace by Jesus Christ - he is Lord of all. That message spread throughout Judea, beginning in Galilee after the baptism that John announced: how God anointed Jesus of Nazareth with the Holy Spirit and with power; how he went about doing good and healing all who were oppressed by the devil, for God was with him." [Acts 10:36-38]

Jesus' Anointing - Spiritual and Physical: Jesus was consecrated and set apart by God as God's chosen Prophet, Priest and King to fulfill the work that God had assigned him to do. As one who was set apart for holy purposes, Jesus, after reading from the Prophet Isaiah's words, was able to say, *"Today this Scripture has been fulfilled in your hearing."* [Luke 4:21]

Jesus knew himself to be the one chosen and set apart by God, anointed and consecrated by the Spirit of God, authorized and empowered by God to preach good news to the poor, heal the sick and release the oppressed. He also set free those who had been in bondage to Satan. He delivered them from the evil one. His was truly an anointed ministry.

Anointed Christians: We have an anointing. If we are to become mature in Christ, then, like Jesus we must know that we have the anointing. It is an anointing that comes not simply from the laying on of hands by others, but from the Holy Spirit that gives us the authority to do that which God calls us to do.

The Holy Spirit gives us birth, grows us up, baptizes us, leads us and empowers us. The Holy Spirit also anoints, consecrates and sets us apart from the common and mundane to be involved in the sacred and holy works of God and God's Kingdom.

The apostle John wrote:
"As for you, the anointing that you received from him abides in you, and so you do not need anyone to teach you. But as his anointing teaches you about all things and is true and is not a lie, and just as it has taught you, abide in him."." [I John 2:27]
Jesus told his disciples:
"Very truly, I tell you, the one who believes in me will also do the works that I do and, in fact, will do greater works than these, because I am going to the Father." [John 14:12-14]

We are authorized by the Spirit of God to do that which Jesus did and to do it in the name of Jesus. We minister under the anointing of the Holy Spirit and in the authority of Jesus' Name. We have the anointing and the authority to preach the Gospel, heal the sick, drive out demons, forgive sins and make disciples for Jesus Christ. [Luke 9, 10; Matthew 28:19]

There are some things that we, as the body of Christ and ministers of the Gospel are **not** anointed and authorized to do. As Believers in Jesus Christ and members of God's Kingdom, we are **not** anointed and authorized to:

- Change God's Word as recorded in Holy Scripture.
    Revelation 22:18, 19
- Substitute other "words or revelations" for God's Word.
    Galatians 1:8, 9
- Alter God's moral and ethical standards established in God's Word.
    Exodus 20:1-17; Matthew 23:36-40
- Change the nature or consequences of sin as defined in God's Word.
    Romans 6:23
- Change God's plan of salvation that is revealed in Scripture, Jesus.
    Acts 4:12

- Preach that "all roads lead to the same goal," or universalism. Jesus is the Way, the Truth and the Life.
    John 14:6
- Change the nature of God's forgiveness and grace, available to all.
    Galatians 2:8
- Preach and teach anything that goes against the character and nature of God as revealed in the life of Jesus Christ. [Hebrews 1:3]

Scripture records the fact that the early disciples *"devoted themselves to the apostles' teaching and fellowship, to the breaking of bread and the prayers."* [Acts 2:42] The apostles taught what Jesus had taught them to teach. He instructed them to teach their hearers to obey everything that he had commanded them. [Matthew 28:20]

We **are** authorized, as were the apostles, to do and say that which Jesus did and said. We are authorized to preach the good news of the Kingdom of God, the Gospel. We are authorized to heal the sick in the Name of Jesus and enable persons to be whole in spirit, mind, body and relationships.

We are authorized to forgive sins in the Name of Jesus [John 20:23]. We are authorized, in the Name of Jesus, to drive out demons and set people free from bondage to Satan. [Luke 9 and 10] We are anointed and authorized to do all those things that enable Jesus, the Son, to bring glory to God the Father.

We must never equate anointing and authority with authoritarianism. Nor is the anointing and authority of the Holy Spirit to be considered synonymous with volume. That is, simply because someone speaks with a loud voice and delivers a message with great power and drama, does not necessarily mean that he or she is anointed by the Holy Spirit. It may mean simply they enjoy being dramatic.

The converse may also be true. Simply because someone speaks in a soft and persuasive tone and delivers their message in a way that would seem to indicate that they are "waiting for the Lord to speak," does not mean that he or she has the Spirit's anointing.

It may, in fact, simply indicate that they have not taken time to prepare for the moment and are hoping that God will give them something to say.

Anointing means that one has been set apart by the Holy Spirit and authorized to carry out the ministry in which they are involved. They are to prepare for and carry out that ministry by the authority of Jesus' Name.

They are Jesus' Ambassador, his representative, his spokesperson. "In Jesus' Name" they have the power to preach the gospel, heal the sick and cast out demons. "In Jesus' Name" they are authorized to forgive sins.

Anointing and authority have to do with the inner knowing that we are under the control and direction of the Holy Spirit and we have the right to be about our Lord's business. And so, we speak or pray or heal or deliver with the confidence that God's perfect Will, will be accomplished in what we are doing.

One dynamic demonstration of the Holy Spirit's anointing and authority is seen in the life of a diminutive Roman Catholic Sister who has a powerful deliverance ministry. She is very effective in helping persons be delivered from the demonic forces that invade their lives.

Her authority is not wrapped up in her stature or the volume of her voice. She simply speaks to the unclean spirits and says, "Shoo, shoo, shoo." And demons flee! She has the anointing and the authority of the Holy Spirit – and the demonic knows it!

She follows the example of her Lord, Jesus. He spoke to the demon, or the sickness, or the fever, or the stormy sea and they obeyed him. He had the anointing and the authority of the Holy Spirit. He did not have to yell. He was authorized by the Spirit of God to be about the work of God. He did not have to assert his authority he had only to use it.

When we work under the anointing and authority of the Holy Spirit, then we see miracles happen as we reach out to anoint others with oil, especially for healing.

I had the privilege of conducting a seminar on healing and wholeness with a congregation, located in Fort Worth. Texas. This dynamic church, called Beautiful Feet Ministries, is near the center of the city and ministers to street people, prostitutes, drug addicts and others who have found themselves in bondage to the things that could and does destroy their lives.

During the Sunday morning service, the sanctuary was filled with people who knew they were safe in that place and knew that the staff was there to love and help them. The staff had proven this through the years.

The pastor invited persons to come forward if they desired prayer for any of their life's needs. One woman came, carrying a child who, six months ago had been born to a crack cocaine addict mother. The child was very small, underweight, frail, and whose arms and legs hung listless, and seemingly lifeless, over my arm as I held him. His tiny body barely reached from the palm of my hand to my elbow. As I looked upon this little child I could feel the heart of God weeping for his people who were lost in darkness.

In the face of the seemingly hopeless circumstances before me, there arose within me a sense of the power and authority of God's Holy Spirit. I felt a strong urge to anoint the child with oil.

As I put oil on my finger and placed it on his head, I simply began to say, "In the Name of Jesus, I anoint you……" and I did not get to finish the statement or "pray" for his healing!

The baby leaped! His arms and legs began to move and kick. His eyes opened. His mouth opened wide and a smile encompassed his angelic little face. He began to laugh and make joyous sounds.

I grabbed him with both hands to keep him from falling to the floor. This baby boy came alive! He was healed.

A hush fell on the congregation for a moment as they tried to assimilate what had happened. Then they broke out in loud shouts and applause. They knew the little child and his mother. They knew it was a hopeless situation for the child because they had seen similar circumstances many times before.

However, God had another plan for that little child. And through him, God gave hope to others and their children who were in bondage. To Him be all the glory!

The Anointed Community of Faith: There is power in the anointing. The early Church went forward in the power of the Holy Spirit, anointed by God and authorized to carry out the work of God's Son to preach the gospel, heal the sick, forgive sins and drive out demons.

If we are to mature and grow up as the Body of Christ and *"attain to the measure of the full stature of Christ,"* then we must likewise use the authority that is given us through the anointing of the Holy Spirit. We do not have to assert our authority. We have only to use it.

As the church, we are the Body of Christ doing the work of Christ in the world. When we "live out" our anointing, we will endeavor to do those things that Jesus did and refrain from doing those things that Jesus refrained from doing and, in the process, experience the abundant life about which he spoke and which he lived.

As Jesus said, *"It is enough for the disciple to be like the teacher and a slave like the master."* [Matthew 10:25]

PERSONAL REFLECTION

Take time to meditate upon the following Scriptures and seek the Holy Spirit's direction as to how these Scriptures may help you understand your anointing.

"As for you, the anointing you received from him remains in you, and you do not need anyone to teach you. But as his anointing teaches you about all things and as that anointing is real, not counterfeit – just as it has taught you, remain in him." [I John 1:27 NIV]

"I tell you the truth, anyone who has faith in me will do what I have been doing. He will do even greater things than these, because I am going to the Father." [John 14:12 NIV]

Reflect on the ways in which Jesus:
- ministered to the lives of those around him in terms of the Gospel he preached,
- related to persons to whom he brought healing,
- delivered persons from bondage to Satan
- forgave people through his spoken word.

Now reflect on how the Holy Spirit anoints and authorizes you to do the same "and even greater things," according to the promise of Jesus.

A TIME TO REMEMBER

1. I have consciously experienced the anointing of the Holy Spirit during the following times:

   _____

2. I especially remember this time when I felt authorized to share the good news of Jesus' love with another person.

   _____

3. This is a time when I was involved in another person's healing.

   _____

4. I was authorized to help an individual experience forgiveness.

   _____

5. In the Name of Jesus, I was able to help a person be delivered from the power of Satan.

   _____

6. This is how I feel when I experience the anointing of the Holy Spirit.

   _____

PRAYER

O Lord God, the God of my Savior, Jesus Christ and the One from whom flows the Holy Spirit. It is my desire to proclaim as did Jesus when he stood before the congregation in Nazareth and read from your Word:

"The Spirit of the Lord is upon me because He has anointed me.
to bring good news to the poor.
He has sent me to proclaim release to the captives,
and recovery of sight to the blind,
to let the oppressed, go free,
to proclaim the year of the Lord's favor."

O God, pour out your Holy Spirit upon my life and anoint me for the work of ministry to which you have called me. May I be as faithful to the task assigned me as Jesus was to his. I humbly ask this in his Name. Amen

CHAPTER 7

RESURRECTED BY THE SPIRIT

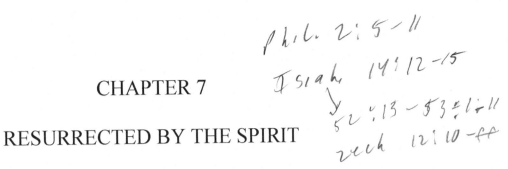

The seventh move of the Holy Spirit in the life of Jesus was to raise him from the dead.

Jesus spent three years of his public ministry under the power and authority of the Holy Spirit. In that power and authority, he taught, healed the sick, forgave sins and delivered persons from bondage to the evil one. In that power and authority, he stood up to those who challenged him. In that power and authority, he taught a standard for Kingdom living that challenged both the righteous and the unrighteous. In that power and authority, he discipled his followers, he suffered opposition, he knelt in the Garden of Gethsemane, he experienced brutal beatings and an excruciating death by crucifixion and suffocation on a cross.

Jesus role-modeled that lifestyle that God had designed for Kingdom living. He was living proof of the resurrection power of the Holy Spirit in every facet of his life and in every event of his life.

Jesus laid down his heavenly glory to become human. Then he laid down his earthly life daily to become an obedient servant of God and humanity. He knew that He had come to earth not to do his own will, but the will of God who sent him. [John 6:38] Therefore, his entire life was one of dying to self so that God's higher purposes for humanity might be realized through him – and that was for humanity to be reconciled with God. [Colossians 1:19, 20]

Each time Jesus died to self, God raised him up. When he humbled himself in the Jordan River baptism experience by identifying with sinful humanity, God raised him up. When he entered the wilderness temptation experience and, in a weakened state, faced his adversary, God raised him up. Ultimately, when he willingly died on the cross at the hands of those who opposed him, God raised him up.

Throughout his life and ministry Jesus put self aside so that God's higher purposes might be realized. Each time God raised him up. He was strengthened, encouraged and empowered by God's Spirit in those times when he denied himself to be God's faithful servant and witness.

He denied himself in order that the spiritual, emotional, physical and relational needs of others could be met. When John the Baptist, Jesus' cousin, was killed, Jesus desired to retreat to a solitary place with his disciples for a time of rest and prayer. However, when he arrived there, a large crowd of people were waiting for him.

Instead of being frustrated because they had intruded on his desire and need for privacy, he responded with compassion. He understood their need. Without complaint, he healed their sick, he taught them about God's Kingdom ad he provided something for them to eat. He took care of the needs of others before his own. [Matthew 14:1-21]

This practice of self-denial was such an integral part of his life that at one point, when he was so busy he couldn't even eat, those around him said that he was "beside himself" or "out of his mind." [Mark 3:20, 21] Yet, this was the nature of Jesus. It was his human lifestyle.

Jesus had truly laid aside his own glory, humbled himself, took on the nature of a servant and became obedient to death. [Philippians 2:6-11] Ultimately, Jesus literally laid down his life as he hung on the Cross.

In all cases, whether in those times when Jesus denied himself so that others might benefit or in the allowing of himself to be crucified, God, by the power of the Holy Spirit, raised him up.

Jesus knew that the same power with which God raised the dead, had been given to him. *"Just as the father raises the dead and gives them life, even so the Son give life to whom he is pleased to give it."* [John 5:21]

During his ministry He used that power to raise certain individuals from the dead. He raised up the widow's son, [Luke 7:12-15] He raised the daughter of Jairus, [Luke 8:49-55] He raised Lazarus, the brother of Martha and Mary. [John 11:43, 44] The resurrection of Lazarus became a major factor in bringing about Jesus' own death, for from that day on the Sanhedrin, or ruling Council, plotted to take Jesus' life. [John 11:53]

Jesus had already declared the fact that there is a resurrection and that there is life after death. The Sadducees, a devout conservative Jewish party who did not believe in resurrection after death, came to Jesus to question him about the resurrection. They presented a hypothetical situation about a woman who had, in turn, married seven brothers, each of whom had died. Since she had been married to each one of them, the Sadducees wanted to know whose wife she would be in the resurrection.

Jesus' response was straightforward and to the point: *"You are in error because you do not know the Scriptures of God. At the resurrection people will neither marry nor be given in marriage, they will be like the angels in heaven. But about the resurrection of the dead – have you not read what God said to you, 'I am the God of Abraham, the God of Isaac, and the God of Jacob?' He is not the God of the dead but of the living."* [Matthew 22:29-31]

Jesus knew resurrection to be a reality and that it ushered in a level and quality of life not known on earth.

Jesus demonstrated in the resurrection experiences for which he was responsible, that he had power over death itself, even though each of those who was raised from the dead ultimately died again. However, in raising Lazarus from the dead he took the opportunity to reveal the fact that death had no hold on him or those who believed in him.

He told Martha, and the others who were close enough to hear, *"I am the resurrection and the life. He who believes in me will live, even though he dies; and whoever lives and believes in me will never die."* [John 11:25, 26]

His pronouncement was soon put to the test. In a very short time he was crucified, fulfilling a prophetic statement he had made earlier that the Son of Man would suffer and die. However, he had also said that after three days he would rise again. [Mark 10:32-34] The proof of his life and the validity of his claims hung on this one declaration. Would he rise again after he died on the cross?

Without the resurrection, his life would have remained as that of other great people who lived good lives, taught sound principles, demonstrated noble lifestyles and died, leaving behind them persons who endeavored to emulate their lives and follow their teachings. The resurrection, however, would show that Jesus really was who he said he was, the very Son of God who had power over life and death. Jesus' resurrection became a reality on the third day after his crucifixion.

On Pentecost, Peter proclaimed: "God raised him from the dead, freeing him from the agony of death, because it was impossible for death to keep its hold on him. *God has raised this Jesus to life and we are all witnesses of the fact."* [Acts 1:23, 24, 32]

Writing about that resurrection in later years, the Apostle Paul stated, *"...Christ died for our sins according to Scriptures, ...he was buried. ...he was raised on the third day according to the Scriptures, and...he appeared to Peter and then to the Twelve. After that, he appeared to more than five hundred of the brothers at the same time, most of whom are still living, though some have fallen asleep. Then he appeared to James, then to all the apostles, and last of all he appeared to me also."* [I Corinthians 15:3-8]

The Holy Spirit moved upon Jesus' life from conception to resurrection. Jesus moved in the power of the Spirit from the time he descended to earth until the time of his ascension to heaven. Scripture reminds us that *"God was pleased to have all his fullness dwell in him, and through him to reconcile to himself all things whether things on earth or things in heaven, by making peace through his blood shed on the cross."* [Colossians 1:19, 20]

Just as God is pleased to have all of God's fullness dwell in Jesus, so Jesus is pleased to have all his fullness dwell in us. God's word reminds us that we are to *"attain to the whole measure of the fullness of Christ and in all things grow up into him who is the Head, that is, Christ."* [Ephesians 4:15] We are challenged to live the life that follows the example of Jesus.

Jesus had told his disciples that it is enough that a student be like their teacher and a servant like their master. His was a life of commitment to doing the will of God. He was committed to denying himself so that others may have life. He was passionate about being an obedient servant so that God's purposes might be fulfilled and so provide a way for the salvation of humanity. We are challenged to follow that example.

The Apostle Paul wrote in his letter to the Christians in Philippi:
"Your attitude should be the same as that of Christ Jesus: Who, being in very nature God, did not consider equality with God something to be grasped, but made himself nothing, taking the very nature of a servant, being made in human likeness. And being found in appearance as a man, he humbled himself and became obedient to death – even death on a cross! Therefore, God exalted him to the highest place and gave him the name that is above every name, that at the name of Jesus every knee should bow, in heaven and on earth, and under the earth, and every tongue confess that Jesus Christ is Lord, to the glory of God the Father." [Philippians 2:5-11]

The only way by which this attitude of Jesus may be accomplished in the life of the disciple of Jesus is through the working of the Holy Spirit upon that life in the same way in which the Spirit worked in the life of Jesus. If we are to experience that resurrection power that Jesus experienced as the Holy Spirit raised him up, then we must be willing to die as Jesus died. Resurrection is a post-death experience!

Scripture clearly establishes that there are indeed two resurrections. First, we must be willing to die to self while we are still alive here on earth. Jesus said at one point in his ministry, *"If anyone would come after me, let him deny himself, take up his cross daily and follow me. For whoever wants to save his life will lost it, but whoever loses his life for me will save it."* [Luke 9: 23, 24]

There are times when we are called upon to deny self or die to self so that the needs of another may be met. What caring person has not faced this issue with their family or neighbors or friends? Parents have sacrificed their own needs for the sake of their children. Teachers have sacrificed their own private time to educate students who have special needs. Persons in the help professions have gone without food and rest to care for another.

Those who are willing to make such sacrifices of their own time energy and needs, find that these personal resources are often replenished beyond what they were originally. Those who have faith in God and who are endeavoring to follow the example of Jesus Christ, discover the supernatural presence of the Holy Spirit who not only replenishes their strength, but gives new life and new joy as well. They discover the truth of Jesus statement that he came in order that we might have abundant life. Abundant life often comes following the denial of self for the sake of another.

When we are faced with potentially life-destroying circumstances – such as abuse or traumatic experiences, the Holy Spirit empowers us to be in control of the circumstances. When the thief, in whatever sin-form, breaks in to steal, kill and destroy that life or relationship that is a gift from God, the Holy Spirit helps us to recognize and overcome the thief. The apostle Paul said:

"If Christ is in you, your body is dead because of sin, yet your spirit is alive because of righteousness. And if the Spirit of him who raised Jesus from the dead is living in you, he who raised Christ from the dead will also give life to your mortal bodies through his Spirit who lives in you." [Romans 8:10, 11]

God's Holy Spirit, who raised Jesus from the dead, gives life to our mortal bodies even as the Spirit gave life to Jesus' mortal body. We do not merely exist, we live!

We are a resurrection people. When we, like Jesus, humble ourselves and die to self, daily, so that the needs of others may be met, the Holy Spirit raises us up. When we are surrounded by circumstances that could rob us of life's joy, the Holy Spirit moves to restore hope, renew trust, increase faith and empower us to confidently hold on to the hand of God.

When we are faced with the physical death experience, we know by faith that we shall not die, for Jesus has already raised us to life. We have already passed from death to life, for whoever lives and believes in Him shall never die. We face the death experience with the faith that we will be raised to new life.

Again, the apostle Paul writes, *"For you died, and your life is now hidden with Christ in God. When Christ, who is your life, appears, then you also will appear with him in glory."* [Colossians 3:3]

The fear of death is no longer an issue because the follower of Jesus knows that he has conquered death and has set free those who all their lives have been in bondage to the fear of death. [Hebrews 1:14, 15]

When Jesus told his disciples that Lazarus' sickness would not end in death, [John 11:14] he knew he was right. Lazarus did die. However, it did not end there. His sickness ended in a resurrection, that brought glory to God and glory to Jesus Christ.

"I have been crucified with Christ, and it is no longer I who live, but it is Christ who lives in me. And the life I now live in the flesh, I live by faith in the Son of God, who loved me and gave himself for me." [Galatians 2:20]

That same resurrection power is present as the Holy Spirit works in our lives. It is the Holy Spirit who helps us *"attain to the fullness of Christ,"* and raises us to abundant life here on earth and eternal life in the heavenly Kingdom of God. It is the Holy Spirit who empowers us to deny ourselves, take up our cross and lay down our lives, following the example of Jesus. It is the Holy Spirit of God who gives us the servant heart and an obedient spirit.

It is the Holy Spirit who *"raises us up"* and enables us to confidently live out our lives as a resurrected people, knowing that death is not the end. We know that the Spirit of God who raised Jesus from the dead lives in us and gives life to us also. Life does not end in death. Rather, death ends in Life!

This working of the Spirit's power was evident in the life of a circus clown. The woman had spent her adult life in clown ministry. She loved to make people laugh. She was convinced of the truth of God's word that *"A cheerful heart is good medicine, but a crushed spirit dries up the bones."* [Proverbs 17:22] She took every opportunity to dress in her clown costume and perform at various gatherings of young people and old alike.

One day she became seriously ill. After consultation with her physician she was placed in the hospital for observation. A medical team determined that exploratory surgery was necessary to discover the cause of the affliction. During the surgery it was discovered that her intestines had become entwined and entangled around each other in a way that could not be corrected by surgery nor successfully treated by medication. The intestines were literally strangling themselves. Foods could not be digested, and body wastes could not pass through the intestines. This resulted in poison passing into her system with the prognosis of death in a few days.

She was placed in a hospital ward and made as comfortable as possible. She wanted more than anything to live. She loved life and she enjoyed helping others to love life. Yet, here she lay, waiting to die.

In the bed next to her lay a woman who had had surgery to correct a malady in her body. The surgery had been successful. Her body parts were now functioning properly, and she could live. Yet, she was dying. She was dying because she had lost her will to live. She could live, yet she wanted to die. She lay in her bed staring straight ahead, never giving any indication that she was aware of anything happening in the room. She appeared to be in a comatose state though wide awake.

Here lay two women, side by side: One wanting to live while her body was in the process of dying; the other wanting to die while her body was prepared to live.

The clown did all that she could to get response from the woman next to her. She believed that if she could just get her to laughing, or move, or communicate then she would experience a desire to live. However, no amount of story-telling jokes, or body motions had any effect. The woman remained locked within herself.

As the clown's energy waned more and more, she knew she had to make another effort to communicate with the woman. With all the energy she could bring forth, she climbed down out of her bed in her hospital gown and crawled on her knees to the end of the other woman's bed so that she could be in her line of vision.

At the end of the bed she placed her head on the floor, braced herself with her hands and lifted her feet into the air. There she stood on her head with legs pointed toward the ceiling.

The other woman saw two naked legs sticking up at the end of her bed. There was an automatic response to such a sight, and she made one sound, "Ha!" With that sound the semi-trance state was broken, and she began to move in her bed.

The clown lowered herself from her upside-down position and crawled back to her own bedside. With her last bit of energy, she pulled herself back into her bed and collapsed. She was totally spent.

The woman in the adjoining bed pushed the nurse-call button. When the surprised nurse came into the room she was even more surprised when the woman spoke and asked for food. She was hungry. The nurse called the medical staff who came immediately to examine the patient and order food for her.

While they were in the room, the clown also asked if she could have something to eat. She informed them that she was also hungry. They were reluctant to give her anything because of her rapidly declining condition and the fact that she could not digest it. However, because of her insistence that she was hungry they gave her food.

Soon each woman's vital signs stabilized, and each began to show improved skin coloration and renewed energy.

The medical team understood what had happened to bring restoration to the woman who occupied the bed next to the clown. Her will to live had been restored through the efforts of the woman next to her.

However, they were puzzled as to why the clown woman continued to improve, even when, according to their original diagnosis, her physical condition was irreparable and irreversible. After much consultation the conclusion to which they came was that as she stood on her head at the foot of the other woman's bed, that very act released the entangled intestines and they returned to their normal configuration. The medical staff had no other explanation. The clown recovered, as did the woman in the bed next to her.

I believe there is a greater explanation for her recovery. The clown woman was willing to use her last bit of energy making effort to help another live. She was willing to lay down her life so that another could live. And, in her willingness to lay down her life, she found life – not only for the other, but for herself as well.

She was following the example of her Lord, Jesus Christ, who laid down his life so that we could live. And, in the laying down of his life he found life – not only for us but for himself as God raised him up.

The seventh move of the Holy Spirit in our lives is to raise us up to eternal life. Death could not hold Jesus. Death cannot hold those who believe and follow Jesus.

"Christ has indeed been raised from the dead, the first fruits of those who have fallen asleep. For since death came through a man, the resurrection of the dead comes also through a man. For as in Adam all die, so in Christ all will be made alive. Just as we have borne the likeness of the earthly man, so shall we bear the likeness of the man from heaven." [I Corinthians 15:20-22, 49]

PERSONAL REFLECTION

Take time to reflect on the following Scriptures and allow the Holy Spirit to reveal the truth of the Scriptures relative to your own life experiences.

1. *"If anyone would come after me, he must deny himself and take up his cross daily and follow me. For whoever wants to save his life will lose it, but whoever loses his life for me will save it."* [Luke 9:23, 24]

2. *"If Christ is in you, your body is dead because of sin, yet your spirit is alive because of righteousness. And if the Spirit of him who raised Jesus from the dead is living in you, he who raised Christ from the dead will also give life to your mortal bodies through his Spirit, who lives in you."* [Romans 8:10, 11]

3. *"I am the resurrection and the life. He who believes in me will live, even though he dies, and whoever lives and believes in me will never die."* [Jon 11:25, 26]

A TIME TO REMEMBER

1. I remember the time[s] when I had opportunity to deny myself and my own needs to help someone else. _____
2. This is how I felt during those times _____
3. The time when I find it easiest to deny myself is when I _____
4. The time when I find it most difficult to deny myself is when _____
5. I remember the time when someone else sacrificed their own needs and comforts for my sake. _____
6. This is how I remember the Holy Spirit "raising me up" when it seemed like everything was lost to me. _____
7. When I am ultimately faced with the experience of physical death, this is how I believe I will respond. _____
8. This is how I interpret "abundant life." _____
9. This is how I interpret "eternal life." _____
10. This is what I believe the resurrection will be _____
11. When I die this is what I want most for people to remember about me: _____
12. Believing that the Holy Spirit has helped me to attain to the whole measure of the fullness of Christ, I desire that my memorial service be one that will celebrate my life in the following way: _____
_____

PRAYER

"Gracious and loving God, you knit me together in my mother's womb. You breathed into me the breath of life and caused me to become a living person.

Through your Son, Jesus you have shown me the way to life abundant and eternal. You have filled me with your Spirit and have enabled me to walk in the way that leads to life.

O, Lord God, forgive me when I am unwilling to deny myself, but instead, elevate myself. Forgive me when I am unwilling to lay down my life so that others may live. Forgive me when I am unwilling to sacrifice for the sake of another.

I desire to be like Jesus and I desire to have your Holy Spirit work in my life as in his. Teach me how to humble myself and take the form of a servant and become obedient to you even to the point of death itself. Help me to know that you have the power to raise me up. Give me the gift of Faith to believe that you will raise me up.

"I thank you for releasing your resurrection power in my life and enabling me to walk as one who already knows eternal life. Thank you for releasing me from the fear of death and causing me to know without doubt that I will never die, for I am yours.

"I commit myself to you from the point of my conception to the day of my resurrection. My whole being is yours. You have bought me with the blood of your Son, Jesus. May your perfect will be done in my life as in his. I pray this in Jesus' Holy Name. Amen"

CHAPTER 8

MATURE IN CHRIST

"...until all of us come to the unity of the faith and of the knowledge of the Son of God, to maturity, to the measure of the full stature of Christ. We must no longer be children, tossed to and fro and blown about by every wind of doctrine, by people's trickery, by their craftiness in deceitful scheming. But speaking the truth in love, we must grow up in every way into him who is the head, into Christ, from whom the whole body, joined and knit together by every ligament with which it is equipped, as each part is working properly promotes the body's growth in building itself up in love." [Ephesians 4:12b]

The Holy Spirit moved in, on and through the life of Jesus from conception to resurrection, enabling Jesus to be and to model the person that God had envisioned all humanity to be.

Jesus was conceived by the Holy Spirit, born of the Spirit, grew in the Spirit, was baptized with the Spirit, led by the Spirit, empowered by the Spirit, anointed by the Spirit and, ultimately, resurrected by the Spirit.

There was never a time when Jesus did not experience the presence of the Holy Spirit in his life – except for that brief time on the cross when he felt totally forsaken by God. He felt the alienated state of the life that is isolated by sin from its Creator.

However, from the time of his Incarnation in the flesh until the time of his Ascension Jesus knew the presence of the Holy Spirit. He obediently followed the leading of the Spirit and fulfilled the ministry of reconciliation that God had given him.

When he said on the cross, *"It is finished!"* He was proclaiming to all creation that his work was complete. God's will for humanity was accomplished. God's own Spirit had carried Jesus through to the finish.

If we, as the body of Christ, individually or corporately, are to become mature in Christ and know the fullness of his life as our own, then I believe we are to call on the Holy Spirit to work in our lives as He worked in Jesus' life. It is God's Holy Spirit who carries us through to the finish.

The Finished Work: As we mature in our faith and in our witness to the world around us, we ultimately move from being disciples [learners] to apostles [messengers]. As the Body of Christ, we become the Beloved Community of Believers that endeavors to make disciples for Jesus Christ by the salvation of souls for the transformation of the world.

Christian maturity is accomplished in the individual Believer's life and in the Community of Faith by the indwelling presence and transforming power of God's Holy Spirit.

It is the Holy Spirit who transforms and changes us into Jesus' likeness. It is the Spirit who helps us attain to the measure of the full stature of Christ and become what God intended for humanity, and the church, to be in the first place.

Jesus said, *"The disciple is not above the teacher nor the slave above the master. It is enough for the disciples to be like the teacher and the slave like the master."* [Matthew 10:24, 25]

"It is finished!" According to God's word, *"The one who began a good work among you will bring it to completion by the day of Jesus Christ."* [Philippians 1:6]

With that in mind, it is good to follow the admonition of the one who recorded the Book of Hebrews:

"Let us also lay aside every weight and the sin that clings so closely and let us run with perseverance the race that is set before us, looking to Jesus the pioneer and perfecter of our faith, who for the sake of the joy that was set before him endured the cross, disregarding its shame, and has taken his seat at the right hand of the throne of God." Hebrews 12:2

Life Application

Special Olympics is a sport for young men and women who may have physical or other restrictions that disqualify them for the Olympic competition that requires the very best of physical athleticism. Yet many can compete at another level and enjoy the spirit of competition among others who experience same or similar physical limitations.

Special Olympics were held in a certain West Coast city and world attention was drawn to what happened in one of the one-hundred-meter races.

The runners positioned themselves at the starting blocks, getting ready for the race. Each was swinging their arms and jumping up and down to relax their bodies.

The person with the starting gun yelled, "To your marks!" The runners all crouched down with hands at the starting line and feet against the starting blocks.

"Get set!" The runners then lifted their buttocks up, ready to begin the race.

"Go!" And with the firing of the starter gun, they began running down the track as fast as their legs would carry them.

Several meters down the race track one of the runners fell. The other runners saw what happened and they all stopped running. They returned to the fallen runner. One of them asked, "What happened?"

The fallen runner said, "I fell."

The others asked, "Are you hurt?"

"Yes."

"Do you want some help?"

"Yes."

The runners helped the fallen person get up. They brushed them off and then they all returned to their lanes, took hands across the lines and one of they yelled, "To your mark, get set, go!" And they all ran the rest of the race holding hands. They all crossed the finished line at the same time and they were all awarded Gold Medals.

It is not known if these young runners were Christian. Nevertheless, it is a perfect example of what life is like when lived with the maturity of Jesus.

By the power of the Holy Spirit we are able, as individuals and as the Body of Christ, to run the race that is set before us, not to outrun our brothers and sisters and get there before they do, but to help the fallen, restore the broken, encourage the weak and run the race together because of the joy that is set before us, eternal life with him who is our Lord and our God.

PERSONAL REFLECTION

1. What are the personality traits in my life that **most** reflect the nature of Jesus Christ? _____

2. What are the personality traits in my life that **least** reflect the nature of Jesus Christ? _____

3. What are some of the areas in my relationship with Jesus in which I feel that I am grown up and mature? _____

4. What are some of the areas in my relationship with Jesus in which I feel that I need to grow up and mature? _____

5. What is my own theology of Christian Growth and Maturity?

PRAYER

"Come, Holy Spirit! Finish your work in me. Make me like my Teacher, Master and Savior, Jesus Christ. In His Name I pray. Amen"

BIBLIOGRAPHY

"All scripture quotations, unless noted otherwise, are taken from the New Revised Standard Version of the Bible, copyright 1989 by the Division of Christian Education of the National Council of the Churches of Christ in the United States of America, Used by permission. All rights reserved."

Wesley Study Bible, New Revised Standard Version
Copyright 2009 by Abingdon Press

The NIV Topical Study Bible, New International Version
Copyright 1989 by The Zondervan Corporation
Grand Rapids, Michigan 49506 U.S.A.

Made in the USA
Columbia, SC
14 October 2018